# will you love me when i'm fat?

a mother and daughter story

patricia rosalind warner

**Will You Love Me When I'm Fat? A Mother and Daughter Story**



ISBN-13: 978-0-692-86474-6



Contact: ToddPondPress@gmail.com

Cover design by Lindy Martin
Cover illustration by Arcangel
Interior design and typeset by Katherine Lloyd

**In Loving Memory**

Robert Ludlow Fowler, III

Charles George Kavanaugh Warner

Nicholas Fish Warner

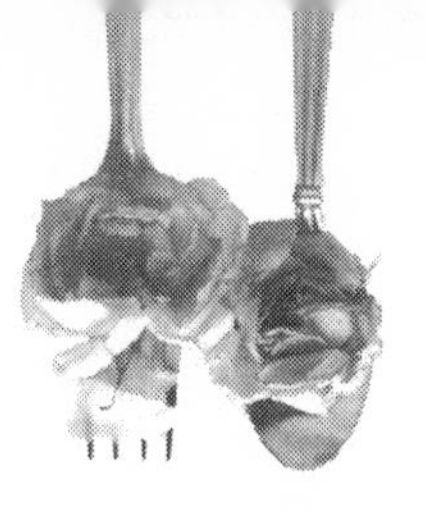

# preface

May 25, 1973, was worse than usual. After switching off the kitchen light and locking the door, I walked up the stairs, bone-tired. I noticed a light under the door of the guest bathroom.

Opening the door slowly, I saw my daughter standing in her underwear, staring at her reflection in a floor-length mirror. A bra hung slackly on her nearly-vanished breasts; her hip bones jutted out like a pair of angled parentheses.

She hunched over in a forlorn attempt to hide. "Mum, will you love me when I'm fat?" she asked quietly, as if it was the most routine of questions.

*Will you love me when I'm fat?*

The words landed in my head like a cannonade, and I squeaked out a reply. "Yes! I will love you when you're fat. I will love you when you're thin. My love doesn't depend on your weight or looks. But can't you see…you're disappearing?"

Thus begins my mother-and-daughter story. How I overcame dark patterns and tragedies in my life so I could help my daughter in the fight of her life. How anorexia nervosa almost killed her. But it also ultimately saved me.

*With my greyhound, Chance*

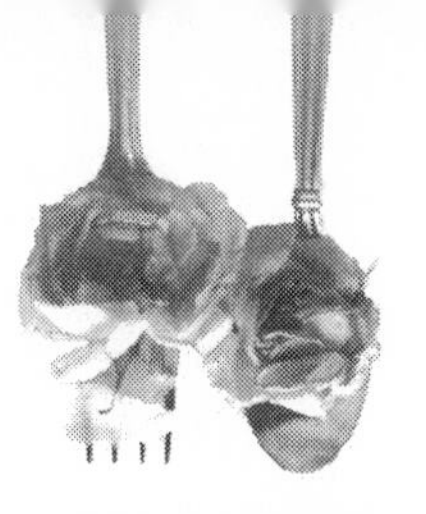

# chapter one

In the latter part of the nineteenth century, my paternal grandfather, George Chalmers Cutler, the owner of a successful lumber business in Bangor, Maine, moved his wife and five sons to the greater Boston area. He was a big-hearted man who embraced the Puritan work ethic and believed in God, education, family, and exercise.

His eldest son, John Wilson Cutler, my father, married Rosalind Fish, my mother, in 1910. Her family roots could be traced back to the beginning of the American nation. Willowy and beautiful, she had masses of dark fluffy hair and cornflower-blue eyes that crinkled in the corners when she smiled.

Their first residence was an apartment on Commonwealth Avenue in Boston. But soon, in search of better salary, my father found a position at E. B. Smith, a Wall Street investment bank. My twin brother Peter and I were born on May 21, 1921, at the old Lying-In Hospital in Stuyvesant Square, which was the former site of my great-grandfather's house and gardens. Two siblings had preceded us, Susan and Jack, and one would follow, Judy.

I grew up in a game-loving, financially secure family with beautiful, high-spirited parents. I was six when I was photographed in Central Park. My face was badly scratched because I had just defended my brother Peter from boys who were trying to steal his new red scooter. Being the sister of a developmentally-challenged brother colored my life. As long as Peter was alive I was part twin, part guardian.

Life was happy, idyllic even, for us Cutler children. There was a brownstone on the Upper East Side of Manhattan, a summer house on the North Shore of Boston, and, later, a farmhouse on the Hudson. There was a yacht and a big car with a jolly chauffeur and a private school called Miss Chapin's, where all the girls wore baggy green serge uniforms and started each day with a hymn and Bible verse. For too long, I thought all children went to a school like mine. I was too self-absorbed to notice that there were no blacks or Jews at my school.

My world began to fall apart in 1929 with the crash of the stock market and the beginning of the Great Depression. I was eight. My father's temper grew more fiery, and his drinking got worse. Often, when I'd come home from Chapin School, my mother would tell me, "Your father has had another bad day. If you're going to be unpleasant, go up to your room." Was I responsible for my father's moods, his drinking and financial losses?

By the time I was nine, our Irish maids were gone, including our governess. Our house in Beverly had been sold, along with the yacht, but a small farmhouse in Garrison on the Hudson River was built, and there we spent time in blissful disarray, much of the confusion generated by my mother, who thrived on a child-packed household. The fact of approaching penury never bothered her. She didn't need the type of security typically associated with money.

But my father changed when his wealth disappeared. For

instance, his diversions became more solitary, such as walks up the craggy hill behind our house or sitting alone on the terrace watching the sun go down over West Point. I would look out my bedroom window and hear the chanting of the Spring Peepers, the mournful call of the whip-poor-will, and there he would be, long after sunset, alone with a drink in his hand and nothing to break his darkness except for the fireflies.

My father spent more time at his club as the banking business crumbled. There were drinking episodes and arguments between my parents late into the night. My mother was afraid I might get caught in the middle—another excuse for always sending me up to my room.

My 1939 school yearbook offers clues about my teenage self, including a scarcely recognizable photograph of me as a bright-eyed, fluffy-haired girl. The caption below it reads:

*Patricia Cutler*
*Known for: Vivaciousness*
*Goal: To be a spy or first female Director of the FBI*
*Likely to be: Diary writer like Samuel Pepys*

I had learned that smiles made everyone happy.

My parents tried to keep us children protected from the plight of most Depression-era Americans. The long line waiting outside the uptown armory for hot soup was outside our orbit, and when we drove each weekend to Garrison, New York, my mother avoided the Hooverville shacks and Harlem. But we knew about suffering from Rory, our cook's brother, who would turn up in the kitchen to eat what was left of our evening meal and the faces of old men selling chestnuts near the 79th Street entrance to Central Park and the shabbily-dressed women with their apple carts and the street musicians playing threadbare little tunes like "O Tannenbaum."

There was an unreality in the years before Pearl Harbor. Despite the mounting war sounds from Europe, my group of friends kept to our routine: college football weekends, coming-out parties, dancing cheek-to-cheek at LaRue's, moviegoing, learning how to smoke while reciting lines from our favorite movie stars—Katharine Hepburn, Clark Gable, Gary Cooper, and Fred Astaire.

In those early years, I didn't understand why my parents and most of their friends hated President Roosevelt. "He sold us down the river" and "He's a traitor to his class" were the themes that rang through my childhood. It was difficult to reconcile the image of a big-hearted man trying to create jobs for the poor with my kind-hearted relatives disliking him so.

My first major act of rebellion was voting for President Roosevelt in 1940. FDR's New Deal meant losses for people of wealth like my father. No one I knew looked deeply beneath the soup kitchen lines, prohibition, or tensions in the home. Money, like sex and death, was rarely discussed in Old New York circles.

This period for my family was one of heightened confrontations on our putting green, our wooden tennis court, and at the dinner table. Fish aunts circled around with their different views on America's intervention in Europe's war. My mother and her sister, Julia, a World War I widow, sided with the British, backing FDR and his controversial Lend-Lease Bill. Mother's oldest sister, Janet, who had served as a volunteer nurse near the Franco-German lines in WWI, was also for early intervention, but her sympathies lay with the French. My mother, who was making serious money at the bridge table by night, contributed a large portion of her winnings to British War Relief, where she worked by day rolling bandages.

In the middle of this Fishery was Uncle Ham. Through my young lens, he was a force of nature with his booming voice, his stature (six feet four inches), and his weight (240 pounds). He could make young children tremble as he must have his opponents on the football gridiron as a two-time Harvard All-American. In World War I, he was captain of a black infantry regiment that spent more time on the front lines than any other American unit and was highly decorated for his service by the French. Elected to Congress at war's end, he became a champion for veteran's rights and a powerful voice for isolation. No entangling alliances or foreign wars were his mantra, and FDR was his arch foe. Despite his many accomplishments, I thought he was lacking in humility and vision. He remained a Far Right Republican and a self-proclaimed patriot until his death at one hundred and two.

The war was going disastrously for the British in 1940. Fire-bombing was intensifying in the cities and children were being evacuated. Three thousand British children came to America, most through official channels, a few through private arrangements. That was how Alistair Horne, a shy, melancholy teenager, walked into our lives. The week before his arrival, Mother told us at supper, "Just think of him as a houseguest with very nice manners."

My aunt met him at the Cunard pier. He was among hundreds of evacuees disembarking from the liner *Britannica.* It was searing hot the next day as they drove 60 miles north on the Merritt Parkway to Garrison Highlands. There was a dark brooding sky, and then a storm struck and hail pelted their car and thunderclaps reverberated through the hills. It was an inauspicious beginning, which Alistair described in his book, *A Bundle from Britain*, which is dedicated to my mother and her sister, Julia Breese.[1] In it, he describes first meeting my mother.

> Out of this Wagnerian scene, emerged a large lady with a shock of greying hair in a dress, which seemed to begin and end nowhere, with great loose sleeves covering her arms, outstretched like the prophet Elijah. I viewed her approach with some concern.

"So this is little Alistair," my mother said (never mind that he was fourteen and exceedingly tall). "Well, I'm just going to call you Ally, and you're going to be my sixth child."

> When she was around with her unshakeable optimism, one somehow knew that all would be well, sooner or later. It wasn't Pearl Harbor or the strategy of Churchill that really brought the irresistible weight of America onto our side—"that of the Brits"—it was women like Rossy Cutler.

Peter was the only one of us who was still living at home. He and Alistair shared a room reluctantly. Alistair told us that in England he had his own private "bed sit." But, over time, his manners improved, especially when my pretty younger sister, Judy, was around. In time, young Alistair adapted to our family's "enthusiastic" ways. He would always maintain that the Cutler family gave him back the childhood he never had.

On December 7, 1941, I went with a friend to a football game at the Polo Grounds. The New York Giants were playing the Brooklyn Dodgers. The atmosphere was brooding. Throughout the game, officials were paged with the same message, "Please call your Washington office. Immediately."

Emerging from the stadium, we heard newspaper hawkers shouting the headline: "American Fleet Sunk at Pearl Harbor."

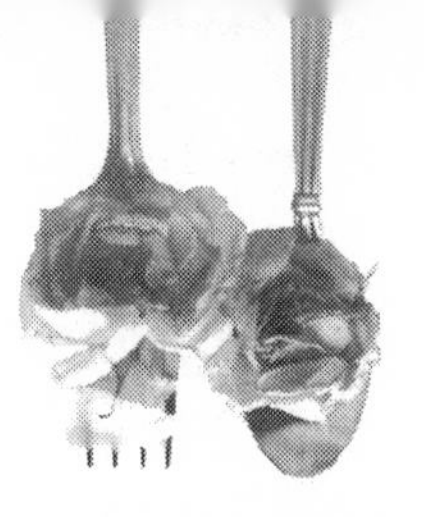

# chapter two

When I think of my childhood, the scenes are mostly sunlit. In the winter, I remember coasting down the old Albany Post Road with Dad looking out for errant cars or dogs. I remember watching "Our Gang" movies on our home projector. On snowy days, the youngest children—Peter, Judy, and I—would walk proudly with our handsome, snowball-throwing father to the RKO 86th' and the silent, black-and-white world of perils and pratfalls. Charlie Chaplin, the Marx brothers, and Harold Lloyd were all I needed to know of the human condition. I wish I could have kept laughing forever.

Looking back at the young girl I once was, I begin to understand the adult I have become. I see myself as an eight-year-old in our house in Garrison, New York, sitting at the top of the stairs gulping for breath between sobs. My Italian greyhound, Chance, had been run over, and I'm dying of my first broken heart. Five years later, I was thirteen and tall for a girl when Mother signed me up for a dance at West Point's Thayer Hotel. She bought me new black patent leather shoes for the occasion.

"Why can't I wear high heels and silk stockings?" I wailed.

*Painting beach scene on Martha's Vineyard while Rob watches*

"Just look at it as a dress rehearsal for the Christmas Junior Holiday Dance."

My mother and all her friends wanted their daughters to meet boys from the best boarding schools, preferably Groton, Andover, or St. Paul's. It was believed that these were the boys who, in time, might be elected to one of Harvard's most prestigious final clubs.

We didn't date just one person, we moved in a group to La Rue, an East 50s nightclub, to New Haven and Cambridge for football games. The Ritz roof in Boston was a big attraction for us New York girls. It was all so wonderful—the parties, dancing to the big bands at debutante balls. In 1939, the year I graduated from St. Timothy's, the Nazis invaded Poland, but we kept on dancing. And sex didn't even enter the picture. My parents knew all the parents of boys I was going out with—beaus, as we called them. There was grappling in rumble seats, movie theaters, that sort of thing. It was the final gasp for the "good girl" era.

Fast-forward six years and I was a twenty-one-year-old newlywed. My husband, Bob Fowler, was a torpedo officer with orders to get his destroyer ready to ship out to the South Pacific. When he was home, he was always playing songs on our Victrola: Cole Porter or "Porgy and Bess." "Pat," he would sing, "You is my woman now."

We were always dancing, sometimes on the town, but mostly at home, wildly around our bed and living room, until the loving began. But our life was tinged with fear that the idyll could shatter at any moment. Both of us knew our farewells could be forever, but we only talked about what our life would be like when the war ended.

After he died, I counted up our evenings together—150. And

for too long after that, I had thought there had been a mistake in the chaos of that shell-filled night off Guadalcanal, that someone else had died, but there was no equivocation in the letter signed by Secretary of the Navy Frank Knox that accompanied his Navy Cross.

I was a war widow with a newborn son.

In 1943, I was living in a New York apartment alone with our son Rob. My days and nights were weighted down with a heaviness I couldn't shake. If only Bobby could have seen Rob with his chubby hands waving in the air.

I thought it was better for my son to have a cheerful nurse than a crying mother, so I hired a nurse and went out looking for a job. A cocoon of sympathy from family and friends surrounded me, but I felt I needed to be working to end the war.

I tried to join the navy, but they wouldn't have me because I had a child. They suggested I try the Office of Strategic Services, the newly formed intelligence agency. The OSS accepted me, and I first went to work as a file clerk in their office in Rockefeller Plaza. After several months, I was shifted to headquarters in Washington for training and then volunteered for overseas duty.

I said good-bye to Rob while he slept in his carriage. I don't think I could have left him had he been awake.

I like to think of myself in the OSS, skulking around darkened bars draped in mascara and allure, dropping truth serum into Nazi officers' champagne. But I'm not sure I made any meaningful contribution to the war effort. However, the time away from home did help me put closure on my grieving for Rob's father.

I was away for seventeen months, and I missed my child every moment. A stream of airmail, tissue-light letters from grandparents and aunts, arrived frequently in my office on Ryder Street in London, documenting in words and snapshots Rob's childhood. I marvel now that I could have left him for even a day. If I'd been familiar with child development and Freudian theories, my choice would have been to stay.

Though the war in Europe was not quite over, my boss in the OSS counterintelligence office in London, Norman Holmes Pearson, a former associate professor of American literature at Yale, felt that I should be home for Rob's second birthday. So I was on my way, carrying a letter that he wrote to my two-year-old son explaining far better than I ever could my reasons for leaving him:

*February 14, 1945—London*

*Dear Rob,*

*Neither you nor I have ever met, but someday I hope we do. The Army Post Office is slow in delivering mail, but probably will never be so slow as when I write this letter and that day in the future when your mother will want to show it to you. Then you will have reached an age when you may wonder why it was that your mother left you when you were a baby, left you with your grandparents, and went off on a mission which her generation and mine shared. It was a mission to make a better world for you to live in... you would know better than we, that it was a task worth trying to affect. For we saw, your mother and I, the horror that faced us in a world in which all honor, all faith in each other, all human decency might be absent.*

*This belief that the world was, and could continue to be, a place of honor and faith and decency, was the belief which made it possible for your father to risk his life and made the losing of it tolerable to those who, like your mother, knew and loved him as a person, or to those who, like myself, respect and loved him as a symbol of the greatness of the human will… When your father died, even as a hero, the necessity for fulfilling his will seemed even greater than ever. I daresay your mother understood him dead even better than he was alive, for death causes a strange maturity in those who do not die; just as she understood the peril of your future even more urgently than she did the helplessness of your minute babyhood. And she was filled—if I understand your mother correctly—with an insatiable urge to complete your father's gesture, and by helping to attain it justify his loss.*

*One had to wonder how one could help best. I know that your mother did help carry out the task which your father gave his life towards attaining, because your mother worked with me and for me, and your mother would willingly have given her life in order to bring the goal about. Your mother has helped to carry us over the hump of the war. It is almost ended now and as her boss I have told her that she should return to you… She has helped make the greatest gift you can have, a world in which the present roots of evil will have been stamped out. At least we have stood our ground. Be proud of your father for having the courage to give up his life for this gift; be equally proud of your mother for having been willing to make this possible.*

*Yours,*
*Norman Holmes Pearson*
*X-2 Bureau Chief, OSS, London*

I worried about what my son would think of me, a pale, skinny woman carrying few presents and trying out my new role as mother. I needn't have worried. Rob accepted me with good grace but limited interest. Apparently, I was not half as entertaining as the two Winnie the Pooh characters I had brought him from London—an oversized stuffed Kanga and baby Roo in her pouch.

We quickly became friends. The nurse left, and Rob and I moved back into our old apartment in the East 80s and started mending the torn fabric of our lives.

That autumn of 1945, I enrolled as a freshman at Barnard College. The months and years that followed formed their own contours for both of us: weekend visits with my in-laws in Katonah, New York, and summer vacations on the Vineyard with my family.

I never felt alone because I had so many good friends and relations close by, but I had a special trip I needed to take.

Rob was four in the summer of 1947 when I embarked alone on a ten-day trip to Hawaii. To come to terms with Bobby's death, I felt I had to see his final burial place at the National Memorial Cemetery of the Pacific in Oahu, which is located in the Punchbowl Crater in Honolulu. Seeing the simple white cross and plaque, I finally accepted his death. I'm not sure if it was my prayers or the rows of white crosses, but slowly over the ten days I spent alone in Hawaii, my grieving abated. What remained was an occasional tug of anger at the Japanese.

Back in civilian life, friends of my late husband were picking up their lives where the war had interrupted them. Many were working in New York City. This once carefree band had grown up understanding that the world "out there" was waiting to receive them with tempting offers of graduate schools, banks, and law offices. No one had spoken to them of emotions, certainly not their parents, whose generation was not far removed from the Victorians.

❦

In the aftermath of the Great Depression, my father had been sick for many years and eventually stopped going to work. As his health deteriorated, it was his brother, Uncle Elliott, a renowned brain surgeon at Peter Bent Brigham Hospital, who took over his case. My father died in 1950 at the age 63, still deeply in debt. After his death, George and Robert, his two younger brothers, both bank presidents, gave valuable financial counsel to my mother.

Family loyalty was an intrinsic part of the Cutler legacy that was passed on down to me. And we all lived on a continuum in which feelings were hidden behind opaque shades of reserve and death was a private matter. The war for me was a watershed in which I lost my childhood. Years later, when my mother was dying of stomach cancer, I wished that death had been something I had learned to talk about. But we were all playing by rules we had learned in childhood.

I was at a cocktail party when I first saw Charles Warner. At war's end, he had lived the Bohemian life on the Left Bank of Paris, hanging out with artist friends at Café des Deux Magots. That night in 1949, he caught my eye, his smoke rings curling upwards until they fitted neatly into one large circle above his head. It seemed to me that a man who could control smoke must have his own sense of direction. He made me laugh—such a gift.

I remember a story Charles told me that evening about his war. He and the men in his company were under shellfire on the Anzio Beachhead when the shelling ceased, and an airplane high overhead filled the sky with whiteness like a blizzard. One flake separated out and grew larger and larger, and fell at his feet. Staring up at him was the familiar face of his grandmother. It was the famous Weegee photograph of Mrs. Kavanaugh and her friend, Lady Decies, emerging from the opera draped in jewels and furs, while a shabbily-clad woman glares at them.

*Yank Soldier: While you are dying at Guadalcanal and Anzio, the opening of the Metropolitan Opera in New York City has never been so glittering and brilliant. All the city turned out to see and be seen, all the famous people were there dressed in the most elegant evening clothes, showing off their favorite jewels.*

Charles well remembered the moment; he was there in uniform, just out of frame of Weegee's camera. Now, thousands of miles from family, they came tumbling out of the sky.

Rob, now almost seven, was rating my beaus, and he ranked Charles at the top. No one else made me laugh the way Charles did, and he planned such grand adventures, like Ringling Bros. Circus or a real Broadway play, like *Where's Charley?* with Ray Bolger. Charles was certainly more fun than that boring Mr. Chadwick, who always brought me white roses and who would sit Rob on his lap and read to him from the *Congressional Record.*

On graduating from Barnard, I won a Fulbright scholarship to study in France, but I didn't want to uproot my son again and the thought of being alone again made me realize that I wanted Charles more than any academic honor.

So, almost seven years after my first marriage, I married again. This time, the wedding was in a small Episcopal Church high above the Hudson River where three generations of my

*Rob and I at my wedding to Charles in 1951 at Garrison, New York*

family had worshipped. Paul Moore, the Anglican priest who performed the service, was a close friend of both my husband's and a godfather to Rob. My father-in-law gave me away. Rob was delighted at the way things were turning out.

For our honeymoon, we went to St. Pierre and Miquelon, islands off the Newfoundland coast. One night, a shrill claxton signaled a ship was in distress and going down in the perilous strait between the two islands. Locals rushed to the rescue, and the crew was saved. The island's alcohol supply vanished in the aftermath, and our peace faded in the bibulous atmosphere of near death on the water. With no lock on our door, we slept fitfully in St. Pierre's only inn for the remaining two days of our honeymoon, our double bed jammed against the door. It was an excessively authentic experience.

When I met Charles, he and his brother Willy were running a ski lodge in Stowe, Vermont, that they called Warner Brothers. I loved the ski lodge but didn't feel it was much of a real job. My banker uncle, Robert Cutler, who was president of Old Colony Trust Company, found him a teller job at the First National Bank of Boston, which lasted a couple of years. Charles had always wanted to teach, so he returned to Columbia and got his PhD in French history. His dissertation, *The Winegrowers of France and the Government Since 1875*, was published in 1960.

*Charles and Cecily*

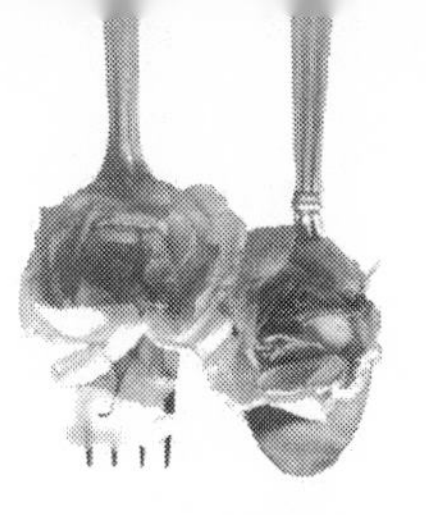

# chapter three

After three boys—one by my first marriage—I finally gave birth to a much-hoped-for girl named Cecily on January 21, 1957. My daughter weighed in at eight pounds two ounces with a birth length of twenty and a half inches, which her pediatrician noted was "entirely normal."

We returned home to our 1920 yellow clapboard home on the corner of Francis Avenue and Irving Street in Cambridge, Massachusetts. My husband was an instructor in humanities at MIT. He was on the lowest rung of the academic ladder, but we were living in the "high brain" area of Cambridge, where our closest neighbors were Julia Childs and Harvard professors, like John Kenneth Galbraith and Arthur Schlesinger.

Cecily took eagerly to her heated formula, and, from the start, her meal hour was in step with the recommended timetable of the famed pediatrician, Dr. Spock. She was a happy, cuddly baby, only crying when wet or hungry. When her needs were met, I would find her cooing, studying a sunbeam or the animal mobile floating lazily above her crib. Marnie, a warm Irish nanny, sang her songs from the "auld country," making the nursery the happy center of family life.

Cecily was eighteen months old when the twins were born. I had wished for a girl, a playmate for her. Instead, I got a pair of look-alikes: a boy we named Josh and a girl we named Roz.

That summer, we rented a house at the beach. This was the summer my older boys, Chris and Nick, discovered entrepreneurship. Unbeknownst to us, they picked vegetables in our neighbor's garden and sold them to another neighbor further down our street. Meanwhile, Cecily was learning about beach life: the way sand crabs skittered along the shoreline and waves snuck up her legs higher than expected and seaweed, dark and slimy, coiled around her ankles. A beach for an eighteen-month-old makes for anxiety but also extremes of happiness. Every day, she wanted to be at the beach, soaking up the marine wonders around her.

My husband's appointment to the MIT Humanities Department ended that year, in May. His next step was as an assistant professor at Middlebury College in Vermont. So, in the fall of 1958, we moved to a rambling farmhouse in the Champlain Valley where, for the first time, I was alone caring for five young children (six when my oldest son, Rob, was home). Au pair girls arrived on the scene, but they usually lasted only a few months; a small New England village is hardly a young foreign girl's American dream.

Our kitchen was Cecily's favorite room. The cabinets were full of exciting treasures at just the right height for a toddler. With a spoon in each hand, her discovery of music began. The orchestral effect she achieved with saucepans and serving spoons made for an innovative kind of atonality. Her taste in music was broad, including nursery rhymes and "Peter and the Wolf" and "Love and Dalliance in Renaissance France."

Most of all, she loved her father's stories. He was a born

teller of tales, spinner of magic. Hearing his Jeep in the driveway, she would run to the back door to greet him, and he would embrace his apple-cheeked Renoir child, bright as silver.

"Daddy, Daddy, 'nother 'tory."

"What is it tonight?" he asked. "The Abenaki Indian legend or the beautiful sisters of the sky?"

"Booful sisters, Daddy."

*The Cat in the Hat*, with its eye-catching illustrations and nonsense rhymes, kick-started Cecily's interest in reading. Her favorite was Beatrix Potter. She loved the stories of little animals and their pursuits—fishing, house cleaning, ironing—and fearsome encounters with Mr. Fox.

Cecily soon knew her favorite stories by heart and "read" them to the twins, skipping over the big words. Sometimes, to be sure of a captive audience, she would climb into the twins' playpen.

We had no TV, and it was rare when a movie worth seeing came to the Middlebury Theater Palace, the most run-down and inadequately heated building in town. Neighbors lived far away and driving was difficult in the winter, so the children were left in charge of their own entertainment.

Cecily loved hiding games. Scrunched into Daddy's closet with the door open, she could hear Daddy's voice getting nearer.

"Where can she be? What a good hider. Maybe she's in Mommy's closet pretending to be a ski boot?"

When the tension became unbearable, a small voice would pipe up, "Daddy, I'm in here!"

Angie Brande, her first true friend, lived on a working farm with a ruddy-faced father and a kindly mother who presided over a kitchen full of pungent baking smells. Cecily felt at home at the Brandes; the noise and warmth of the farmhouse were seductive.

Living with many brothers, she knew boy-girl differences, but she was more interested in the kittens that were born in her bureau drawer. I have a faded snapshot that shows a laughing child with golden-brown hair holding a large white rabbit.

She did not like cows because they followed her too closely on walks through the back pasture. She would never get near to Billy Goats Gruff because she knew goats would eat almost everything. She hated lightning and thunderstorms and dim, poorly-lit corners of the house. And she hated being teased by her brothers.

One day in early fall, Charles returned from Lake Champlain with a brace of wild doves. Cecily, tear-edged and accusatory, pummeled the back of his legs. "Daddy, you killed the bird of peace!" Sensitivity on behalf of the voiceless was an early hallmark of our daughter.

Cecily's nursery school was behind the town library. She was excited about going to school but was also apprehensive. For the first few days, she stuck close to her teacher, but after a week or so, she was joining the other children in games of London Bridge and musical chairs. How grown up she felt, pulling on her snowsuit and big red boots before going off in the Jeep with her father each morning, both on their way to school.

At lunchtime, she had Nick to herself. Chris spent the entire day at his one-room schoolhouse while the twins napped. During lunch, Nick would show her how to draw stick figures and make letters and words.

*Cecily, Josh and Mootsie at Homesite Farm in Vermont*

It was always snowing in Vermont. Fat wet flakes filled the view west to the Adirondacks and we were always in the big kitchen, the warmest room in the house.

Often when the telephone rang, Charles asked me to get it because he thought it might be his mother. "Hello," I would answer. "Nammie? How are you? Oh dear, you've got a cold. I'm so sorry. No, he's not here. Yes, I'll tell him to wear his boots if he goes out today." After eight years of marriage, I knew how emotion-packed conversations between him and his mother could be.

Winter was a happy time for our young brood—one filled with tobogganing, skiing, skating, building igloos, and making snow angels. In the spring, after the "mud season," we would head for the woods and search for the elusive morel mushroom. "Look for the pitted cap!" the children yelled to one another. I often cooked a mushroom recipe for dinner. The *agaricus arvensis* thinly sliced and sautéed with tarragon and shallots was a favorite of mine.

"This new enthusiasm of yours, Pat, is gastronomical Russian roulette," Charles would say darkly when faced with a mushroom casserole.

When I asked Charles later about this time, he remembered me always being in a wicket position surrounded by young—helping with ski boot laces or searching for fiddleheads by Otter Creek.

He loved the "midgets" (Charles's term for the children), but one at a time. Telling Cecily Abenaki Indian legends or trout fishing with Nick was a joy for him, but doing anything with all five barely verbal midgets was a scenario for disaster.

At the Christmas party for faculty children, an annual affair at Middlebury College, Charles was a convincing Santa Claus with his hearty ho-ho-hos as he pulled presents from his bulging sack. Cecily shattered the illusion when she cried out in her fluty three-year-old treble, "Santa's wearing Daddy's boots!"

Chris and Nick were angry at her on the drive home. "Why did you have to say anything about the boots!"

Silence. Then muffled, sniffled words. "But it *was* Daddy. I didn't think—"

"You never think!"

A blast of freezing snow tore at the car as Charles bellowed from the front seat, "Quiet everyone, or we'll spend the night in the ditch!"

By late December, Charles was already tired of winter and the mock jollity of the Christmas season. He was annoyed he had agreed to play Santa. "They'll have to find another Santa next year," he said.

My husband was a worrier. He worried about accidents, about mushrooms that might be poisonous, about temperamental Christmas lights. He worried about almost everything when the children were young. He was a professor, and what he needed was time alone to think, write, and prepare for his next lecture.

One lunch stands out in my memory. I was in the kitchen cooking hamburger casserole when he returned home from his morning class. The long kitchen table was set for lunch. The twins were in their high chairs, separated by Cecily, cherubic and content in her role as peacemaker.

When there was spilled milk or other atrocities by the twins, she would cheerfully remind anyone, "They're only babies, you know."

Chris would blurt out, "I'd like to know when they'll stop being babies."

Charles, tired of sibling warfare, would say in his sternest voice that he wished to "elevate the conversation." He was always trying to elevate the conversation.

The frail health of our hundred-year-old farmhouse was always a problem. The pipes would freeze. The pump in the cellar had to be monitored constantly during spring thaws. The primitive septic tank drained into an open ditch. Charles knew his Jeep wouldn't start on really cold mornings and the town plow would block our driveway with a hard pack of snow after a winter storm.

Charles's idealized picture of Vermont life was slowly losing its glow. Where were the children, scrubbed and tidy in their footed pajamas eager to help with the evening chores? Where was the wife he knew—the one who once looked like Katherine Hepburn—and now was barely recognizable in heavy pants and layered sweaters?

With an au pair to handle the late-night feedings, Charles could usually forget his grievances when I joined him in bed. But the nights I was on double duty, one hour feeding time for each baby, I was too tired for intimacies, too tired to even get undressed for bed.

What Charles enjoyed most about Vermont—duck hunting on Lake Champlain, walking in the woods after snows had melted, trout fishing, and local politics—were outweighed in his mind by the endless winters, the draughty house, and demands from the college. The teaching load was bad enough, but chaperoning fraternity house parties and woodsman weekends at the Breadloaf campus was getting to be too much.

I'm not sure if it was the frozen pipes or a deeper questing, but one day Charles submitted his request for a leave of absence from Middlebury. We sold Homesite Farm, including the house, barn, and all one hundred acres, and moved back to Cambridge.

That summer, I took a Harvard Extension School course in remedial reading and then, in the fall, taught part-time at the twins' school.

"How are you doing with them?" Charles asked me one day.

"Better," I answered. "They're confused by the left-to-right sequence of letters. But they're starting to get it."

The slightly glazed look on his face reminded me that my enthusiasms were not always the same as his. "This place looks like we just moved in," Charles would say, referring to the seasonal rotation of athletic equipment in our front hall, library books piled high on chairs and clothes from the cleaner hanging on backs of sofas.

I was busy with our children but also an avid painter deep into the Boston art world. I showed a few of my paintings around town and was a board member of the Institute of Contemporary Art. In the summer of 1954, one of my still lifes was selected by the jury of the Boston Arts Festival for an exhibition on the Boston Common.

Another exciting moment that spring was being invited to a White House dinner honoring my uncle, Robert Cutler, who was leaving his position as the first director of the National Security Council. President Eisenhower and the First Lady hosted a mix of guest, mostly our family and friends from Boston. Toasts were plentiful. At one point, the president presented one of his paintings to my uncle. It was a painting of a mill and waterwheel in a gold frame with an inscription reading, "To Bobby Cutler from D.D.E, March 12, 1955."

Charles was appointed associate professor at Middlebury College, so he had to return to Middlebury for one more academic year.

Cecily skipped a grade, and that September, at the age of seven, she entered third grade at Shady Hill School. The twins were starting to separate, and by the end of that academic year, they had discarded their private twin talk. I found a warm, bouncy English girl to help with the children. Cecily would remember her fondly. She took Cecily to her first meal at a restaurant. It was Polynesian, full of candlelight and strange, sweet smells. They took a subway to get there.

Starting with nursery school, Cecily's school reports were excellent. Her homeroom teacher in third grade wrote, *Cecily is a very outgoing child. She has a creative mind and vivid imagination. She has been very cooperative and a good student in all subjects. It is a pleasure to have her in class.*

But then, one year later, I received a different note:

> *Cecily has had a successful year in the fourth grade. She is young for her group, but she is such an intelligent girl that her grade placement is correct. She has tried to meet my requirements for her and has been very cooperative and responsive in her work. Immaturity shows away from the classroom, in sports and in her eager desire to please her classmates. She is a sensitive and gifted child with tremendous promise.*

Cecily was preoccupied with her social life. Her image was of the cheerful, well-adjusted child. I assumed she would move through life's stages without missing a step.

In the fourth grade, her class studied Greek civilization. The final in late May was known to Shady Hillers as the Olympic

Games. I have a photograph of Cecily standing beside a hand-painted Greek shield, a round-faced girl, hair falling thickly to her shoulders, smiling as if she had just carried the torch to the top of Mount Olympus. Cecily recalled her Shady Hill years as the happiest of her academic life.

She would tag along with Chris to Boston Red Sox games. She kept lists of Red Sox players and their stats. Carl Yastrzemski and Tony Conigliaro were as glorious and powerful to her as Greek gods.

She had started taking violin lessons while we were in Vermont. When practice went well, she wanted to be a professional violinist. For two summers, she and her friend Angie Brande, both members of the young Green Mountain Fiddle Group, spent three weeks at Bennington College, where they played violin by day and attended rehearsals of the Vermont Symphony by night. She loved those Bennington summers and pleaded with us each year to let her return.

Charles was the very image of the well-ordered man, setting out each morning for the stacks of Widener Library in Harvard Yard carrying a briefcase filled with notes on French agrarian policy. But Cambridge, or maybe Charles's place in it, had changed in the six years we'd been gone. Before, when he was teaching at MIT, life had a definite shape. Weekends and free time were filled with nonacademic pursuits. Now, with MIT and Middlebury behind him, what was ahead? Living in Cambridge and not being part of the Harvard community made him feel like a failure. The atmosphere of the university wove its tendrils around the minutiae of his daily life and began to grate on him, eroding his self-confidence. A lunchtime martini with a twist was a crutch.

Charles needed a teaching position, but there weren't any openings for French historians in the Boston area. Taking another teaching job would mean moving again, but he was hesitant about another uprooting. One evening, he told me about an opening in Iowa. He spread an array of books on the coffee table—Frederick Jackson Turner's *The Significance of the Frontier in American* History and Willa Cather's *O Pioneers* and *My Antonia*. I still remember the drawing on the book jacket of *Sod and Stubble*, a man plowing behind a pair of yoked oxen while a threatening sky looms.

"It's a pure teaching job. No committee work. Just graduate students and good pay," he told me. "Alan Steere is going on sabbatical, so I'll be filling in for him just for a year. His wife will tell you about schools."

For me, an Easterner who had never been west of the Hudson (except for four weeks on a Wyoming ranch one summer), the Hawkeye State was a new and different world. I pictured a landscape of freshly painted farm buildings in a cottonwood grove, black soil, and rows of corn standing straight and unbending like Grant Wood characters.

Chris and Nick were very clear about *not* wanting to move again. They both loved their Cambridge schools and friends. For Nick, it was the art studio at Shady Hill; for Chris, the world of ice hockey. We started to research boarding schools. Rob was in New York City, where he had a job at CBS, so only the twins and Cecily moved to Iowa with us.

I worried how the move would affect Charles's drinking, which was getting worse. Would he be less interested in the lunchtime martini in a different city? I hoped for a geographic cure.

*Portrait of the Warner family in Cambridge, Massachusetts*

*Cecily at riding camp*

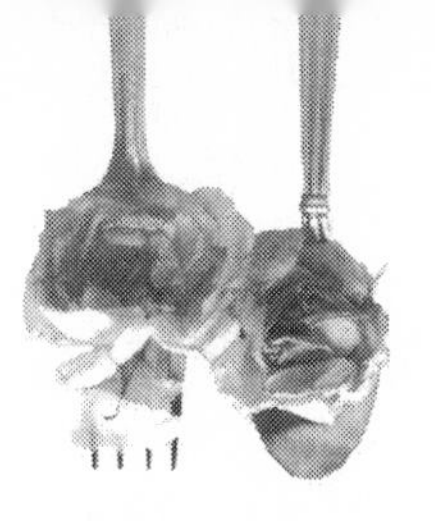

# chapter four

In a journal entry dated May 1966, I described our new life in Iowa:

*Our house, very small, near huge teaching hospital, came completely furnished. Only had to bring our clothes and children's favorite possessions. Charles happy at University, enjoys colleagues and students. Says this is the best year ever … ever. He has made friends among the native Iowans through AA meetings, plus academes from different disciplines. We love our weekend excursions to places often along the Mississippi River. Sometimes as far north as Dubuque, a city of hills and cable cars quite like San Francisco. Driving in any direction through the lush and orderly countryside is an aesthetic experience.*

*A doctor's family with three children lives next door. Mrs. Hunt is from Kentucky, friendly and fond of sharing her Southern recipes. The children get along nicely and most afternoons play together on the hill in back of our two houses. There is a girl same age as Roz and a boy with musical interests right for Cecily. They quite often practice the violin together. The sisters have been sharing a bedroom—lots of giggling and whispering at night.*

Roz steered her Flexible Flyer sled into a tree that winter. She hit the tree head on, ending up with a skull fracture, threatened eyesight, and deep facial cuts. An ambulance sped her to the intensive care unit of Iowa City Hospital. Her right eye was swollen shut, and she couldn't talk because the accident had jarred her teeth loose. Everyone in her class wrote to her. She received twenty-three cards and letters of sympathy!

The next year, Charles got a job at the University of Kansas. We moved to Lawrence, Kansas, in August 1967. All I knew of Kansas was the little I remembered from American history classes and a movie of W. C. Fields dropping into a jungle clearing in darkest Africa and saying to an authentic-looking cannibal, "Tell me, good man, are we in Kansas City, Kansas, or Kansas City, Missouri?"

Cecily loved her room in our new house. It was filled with morning sun and big enough for all her animals, alive and stuffed. There was even an extra bed for a friend.

Cecily was in the sixth grade at the Hillcrest Elementary School, which was three blocks from our house. Her teacher, Mrs. Teebolt, was always telling the class about the medical disasters that occurred regularly in her family. Outside reading was not encouraged. They had workbooks to get through and questions to answer to demonstrate they had done the reading. Mrs. Teebolt fired off directions like a drill sergeant, except when fathers came to class on visiting day. Then she would put on her Doris Day voice and a blue velvet dress with matching shoes. "Mum, she is so fake," Cecily said.

One day, the school nurse invited mothers and daughters for a talk and movie about growing up. It was the worst thing Cecily could imagine, sitting next to me and looking at something as gross as reproductive organs. She tossed the invitation in a litter basket on the way home.

The first two years in Kansas, there was much to enjoy. Cecily had her friends, music, riding lessons, and *Alice in Wonderland*. Here was a heroine she could identify with, not a princess to be awakened, but a polite girl trying to please, wise and curious. All those extraordinary characters were real for her. Nothing was as exciting to Cecily as the nights we went to the opera in Kansas City. She would get dressed up and dab herself in perfume. We would eat at her favorite restaurant and bask in the enchantment of "Tales of Hoffmann," "La Traviata," "La Bohème."

Nancy Golden was Cecily's best friend in Lawrence. Taller and thinner than Cecily, she had long brown hair and dark, deep-set eyes. Cecily's fascination with Nancy began with her mother, who ran an ice-cream parlor on 9th Street with a candy-striped awning that served fourteen flavors. The girls would head there after school and sit at the counter on white wrought-iron stools, transfixed by all the choices.

On weekends, Nancy often came for sleepovers. The two girls lined up their favorite records and played them late into the night—"I Want to Hold Your Hand," "Yellow Submarine," "Eleanor Rigby," "A Hard Day's Night."

I was upstairs in my room one night when I heard Nancy ask, "Who is that?"

"That's my half brother's father. He was killed in World War II."

They were looking through an old family photo album. I

knew the photograph they were looking at—a handsome man in the courtyard of his family's house. There was a photo of me on the opposite page standing with a bottle of champagne in my hand and a huge warship looming in the background. Cecily said with wonder in her voice, "That bottle has real champagne in it!" In the quiet that followed, I imagined the feelings of two ten-year-old girls as they grappled with the concept of loss. They knew how it felt when their favorite pet died, but not a laughing young man just married and leaving a young wife behind.

From an early age, Cecily took pride in keeping her room clean. She arranged her stuffed animals in a perfect row along her pillows and stacked her books and records neatly on a shelf. By the age of eleven, though, she was finding reasons to be doing something else. There were so many animals to take care of, hamsters who escaped, turtles with colds. Cecily loved all animals, but none more than her Siamese cat, Nu-Dang. Nu-Dang followed her everywhere.

Cecily began spending days in her bedroom, leafing through fashion magazines, writing in her diary, making long lists of friends and their unique characteristics. When she deigned to be with us, it was for dinner or a game of Scrabble. The writers she had once loved—C. S. Lewis, George MacDonald, and J. R. R. Tolkien—were replaced by Herman Hesse and Carlos Castaneda. She read her brother's copy of *Steppenwolf.*

During this time, Cecily began piano lessons. At a recital that summer, Cecily played the first movement of a Beethoven sonata and a Schubert theme. After a break for refreshments, she and her teacher sat at matching baby grands to run through a jazzy rendition of Scott Joplin, Cole Porter, and George

Gershwin tunes. For Christmas that year, Cecily gave me a cassette of the recital, a tangible memory of a special afternoon.

My daughter, as a teenager in transition, was caught between the world of children and the world of adults, and she was growing quieter by the day. She wanted to be grown up and brave. She wanted her brothers to admire her, but somehow she just annoyed them. She would remember how mad they got at the Christmas party in Middlebury and Daddy's boots. She didn't want to know that Santa was really Daddy. She wanted Santa to be Santa. She was slowly learning there was pain with the end of things.

Many activities that used to be fun for Cecily were now boring or unpleasant. While her friends headed to the main teenage part of Weaver's Department Store, Cecily shopped in the "chubby" section. The saleswoman had blue hair and a mouthful of gold fillings that gave her voice a ringing, metallic tone, carrying her pronouncements to all corners of the floor—"Here's a 32 cup, dear. Very firming and flattering."

"It's just baby fat getting redistributed," I told her. "In a few years, it'll be gone."

We drove the long way home after those shopping trips so we could stop at Mrs. Golden's ice cream store.

Gym was required of everyone at West Junior High. Cecily hated undressing in the locker room. She hated her new bra and envied the girls who wore their bras proudly. Her best friends—Kimberly, Sarah, and Wendy—seemed far more together. They could put on nail polish without smearing it and knew which bell-bottoms to wear.

She telephoned friends wanting to know about oily foreheads or what to wear to school. She thought if she had had an older sister, she would have known everything worth knowing, but she only had a younger sister who didn't know anything. Now, Cecily preferred to be alone, galloping on her rented horse, Midnight, or playing Mendelssohn on her violin.

She loved it when her grandmother came to visit. Traces of my mother's Gibson-girl beauty were still visible. Mootsie, as we all called her, would sit in a big yellow armchair waiting for her granddaughter to come home from school. Then she and Cecily would play checkers or backgammon.

"Please, Mootsie, tell me a story," Cecily would implore.

She loved the tales that linked her grandmother to the glamorous, glittering world of Newport and people who lived in houses as big as palaces. She knew the stories of dinner parties where ladies received jewels as favors and the orchestra played through the night. She would close her eyes and imagine her grandmother in a short, straight silver dress, aflame with sequins and allure. But when she opened them, there was Mootsie in a baggy skirt and blouse shaped like a pillowcase with gray hair that looked as if it had been frothed up in a Waring blender.

"Mootsie, Mootsie, tell me about the monkey party again?"

My mother was delighted to have a captive audience. "Well, long, long ago when I was growing up in New York City, my mother died very young, but an aunt took great interest in me. She was wonderfully amusing and loved to tease and make fun."

"When are we getting to the good part?"

"Anyway, one day Aunt Mamie sent out invitations announcing a formal dinner party at her house in honor of the Prince del Drago. For weeks, all anyone in Newport could talk about was this mysterious prince. They all wondered which royal house in Europe he descended from. Aunt Mamie refused to divulge her secret. And no one guessed." Mootsie would pause in her story, and Cecily's eyes would widen. "Well, on the night of the party, anticipation was high as the prince was about to make his entrance. You can only imagine their feelings when down the marble staircase on the arm of Mrs. Stuyvesant Fish came a monkey wearing a tuxedo." Mootsie stopped and sniffed. "I smell rosemary, onions, and shepherd's pie."

"Mootsie!" Cecily wailed, "this's the best part!"

So her grandmother continued, "Through four courses the prince behaved beautifully until the dessert. An ice cream flambé was brought in." Mootsie paused again.

Cecily completed the sentence. "And then he went back to his monkey ways!"

"Exactly! He leapt onto the chandelier and began pelting the guests below with tiny light bulbs!"

After her grandmother's stories, TV didn't interest Cecily. She thought *Gilligan's Island* was "dumb," but she loved romantic movies like *Gone with the Wind*, *Romeo and Juliet*, and *Doctor Zhivago*.

She bought fashion magazines at Raney's Drugstore and lingered over articles about "the seductive feel of mink" or "how to lose 10 pounds in a week." She studied the tall, willowy models in clothes from Bergdorf Goodman and Henri Bendel. She worried that all the models looked slim and long-legged like her mother, while she looked so chunky and ordinary. All those beautiful wasp-waisted women with their carefully made-up faces and shining hair and Pepsodent smiles were from a place far away from Kansas and cheerleading and Saturday night movies at the Hillcrest Shopping Plaza.

She wished we had subscriptions to *Glamour* or *Vogue* instead of The *New Yorker* and *The Hudson Review*. She had a subscription to *National Geographic* and especially enjoyed the story of Hope Cook, the American girl who visited Darjeeling and met a crown prince from Sikkim, and then she married him and became the Consort of Deities. The article had a picture of the royal couple with their young son. Hope looked oriental and romantic. Cecily wondered if a Consorts of Deities felt different than ordinary people.

Slowly, very slowly, her self-esteem was chipping away. She had trouble identifying with anyone she knew. Among her more popular friends, she felt like a visitor in her own skin, clumsy in her gym suit—especially when it was her turn at bat or on the vaulting horse.

Spring in Kansas in 1968 came suddenly on puffs of warm and lilac-scented air. I opened the kitchen windows, and, as I looked out over our front yard, I heard the slurred whistles of an early cardinal. Three blocks from our house, the town stopped suddenly and the fields of sorghum began. Spring had always been my favorite time of year, but this year there was a charge in the air in Lawrence and other college towns.

I was working toward a graduate degree in special ed and teaching part-time in a community college in Kansas City when Charles pulled me aside. "Listen, Pat, I don't want you going to these ROTC protest marches. There's a lot of anger in town and on campus."

"I want to finish this term, then I promise I'll stay off the barricades," I told him jokingly.

It was not a laughing matter when I joined the march in Selma, Alabama, for black voter rights in 1965. Charles recalled the incredulous voice of his mother-in-law: "You mean she's in Selma marching? How could you let that happen?" Charles had not tried to stop me then, but, seeing me hovering on the edge of active involvement again, he didn't like it.

"This town is still segregated—houses, restaurants, jobs," I said. "Have you seen those shacks along the Kansas River? No one should have to live like that."

"I'm for change, but in an orderly way," he said. "The condition of blacks is lousy and we shouldn't be in Vietnam, but protests won't solve anything." I remembered one of his Middlebury College lectures I attended. His deep study of the French Revolution gave him a dispassionate perspective in which meaningful change evolved through slow organic growth, often taking centuries. He was talking in a "what if" style. He saw pageantry and rituals as stabilizing forces, visible symbols standing up against political anarchy. But the men elected to the French Assembly had their own agendas but were unable to control the forces they unleashed, leading to the destruction of the Bastille, the Reign of Terror, and the guillotine.

I guess I was smiling at him.

"What's so funny?" he asked.

"You're in your Brooks Brothers suit when most of your colleagues look as unconventional as their students."

He muttered something about keeping up standards. "When the process starts to break down, it's hard to contain. The agitation is spreading into high schools. Even the junior high's getting bomb threats."

I mentioned I'd seen Cecily and some of her friends down by the rooming houses where the protesters were camping out.

"They're mostly stoned so not much of a threat," Charles said.

"Is it worse here than on other campuses?" I asked. "Or does it just feel that way because we're in the thick of it?"

"Ozzie Backus told me he saw you walking with the students in last week's antiwar march." Ozzie Backus was a professor of

Russian history. I did omit mentioning some of my activities. I was taking classes on campus and tutoring a dyslexic black child from North Lawrence.

When I think of the late sixties, I hear the noise of the counterculture, the turned-up sounds of the Rolling Stones and Bob Dylan. Peter Fonda in *Easy Rider* peered from a poster in my son's bedroom. How can children believe in our values when they hear Mick Jagger in his silver suit proclaiming, "I can't get no satisfaction?" How can they believe in a 9-to-5 work ethic when they read Jack Kerouac's *On the Road*? No beds to make, no responsibilities—what nirvana to be the questing teenager.

Charles wasn't the kind of father who enjoyed the bottle-diaper stage. When the children got older, he became more involved and was more ready to show affection. But it upset him to see his older sons moving with the antiauthority wave of the sixties. Cecily witnessed the angry, escalating scenes between her brothers and her father and often tried to intercede.

The new-age feelings in our house were not contained to the boys' rooms at the end of the hall. One day, I found marijuana growing in my border garden.

Chris kept a journal in which he lashed out against American authority figures, including politicians, police, and *fathers*.

Charles, who was always on the side of authority, would counter, "The police are just doing their job, Chris."

"Sure, just like they did in Chicago."

Often, communication would snap with visceral anger, and I would find myself in the middle, trying to explain my husband to our children. War was firmly back in my world, triggering the painful memory of the wartime death of my first husband. Protesting felt like a natural path for me, but I had no idea that, by avoiding an honest discussion with my husband, I was setting the stage for what was to follow.

I did fight with him about Chris's choice of where he wanted to finish his high school, the Windsor Mountain School in Lenox, Massachusetts, a place with a courageous headmaster, a liberal educational philosophy, and a good hockey team.

Cecily and the twins were allowed the freedom to roam the town and campus during our first year in Lawrence, but, starting in 1968, I wanted to know their plans at breakfast.

"Cecily, it's okay if you're going to a friend's house after school, but check in with me when you get there. The campus situation is very tense right now."

One day, it was announced in our local paper that antiwar activist Abbie Hoffman was coming to speak at KU. Many of Cecily's friends were planning to attend, but Charles and I didn't think it was a good idea for her to go.

"The police think there may be trouble, and they don't need their job complicated by the junior high contingent," I told her.

"But Kim and Sarah are going!" she protested.

"They're a year older."

Charles broke in, "You're not going. That's final!"

We had showed Cecily several boarding school catalogues—beautiful ivy-covered buildings, lovely open fields, scrubbed girls in uniform looking happy.

"Would you like to look at schools?" I asked her one day.

"Mmm…I guess so."

I was pushing for St. Timothy's, a school outside Baltimore that I had attended happily.

"An all-girls' boarding school will give her time to grow up slowly away from the pressures of dating," Charles said. He had seen one of Cecily's friends with a boy driving into the Colonel

Sanders parking lot on 23rd Street. The girl was fourteen months older than Cecily and seemed extremely worldly wise.

"Cecily's a year younger than most of her friends," I reminded Charles. "That's why she acts less sophisticated. I'd hate for peer pressure to push her into a situation she's not ready for." An all-girls church school did seem to be a safe place for slow maturing.

"At least she'll be far away from all the unrest on campus," he added.

Boarding schools were a rite of passage among the children of our friends. Over the years, the young survived very nicely, even loved their schools, as Charles and I had.

It was soon good-bye to Kansas and its big sky and tornado watches, good-bye to friends with braces and freckles, good-bye to towering grain elevators down by the railroad where sunflowers grew like small trees.

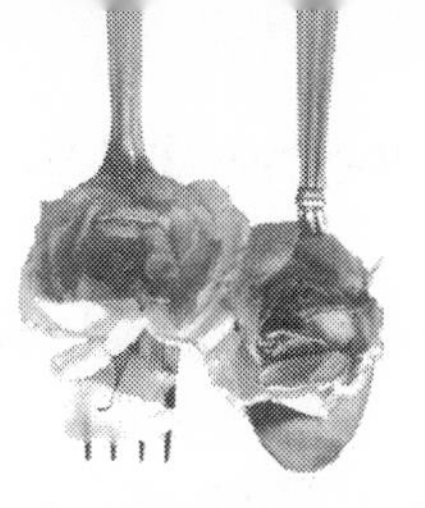

# chapter five

The summer of 1970 was a good time to be out of the country. Most of Charles's colleagues had spent far more time on research projects in France than Charles.

"How would it be," he said one morning, "if I go over early? That way I can get started on my research, and you can bring the children over in June when their school gets out."

Charles had found a small stone house 27 miles northeast of Paris in a town called Senlis, which was an easy commute into Paris and the Bibliothèque nationale de France. Our lovely formal garden was spread with roses, jasmine, and flowering fruit trees. We looked over the high Roman-Gallo walls to the cathedral spires in the older section of town.

Charles and I thought Senlis was intoxicatingly beautiful. Each morning, we passed through a heavy gate down a winding cobblestone street to buy baguettes and watch the carts come in from the surrounding countryside with produce. We watched the local children playing in the square near the cathedral. Some days, Cecily brought back rabbits she rescued from certain culinary demise. By the time we left Senlis, we had to find homes for a large menagerie.

In the evenings, we would watch a funny cartoon program, *Les Shadoks*, and afterwards Cecily would write in her diary or letters to her friends back home in Lawrence. Though she was the child who was most interested in the culture and history of France, she was also the one who missed Kansas the most.

Cecily's diary from Senlis, June 1970:

*Now I will try and tell you about my family. Roz tries to act and dress like a revolutionary, but she's just a copy of Chris and Nick and their musical tastes and words, but she doesn't read books that inform her about the revolution. She won't even listen to stuff like Stravinsky or Debussy. She is funny and nice and natural.*

*Nick is very cute and nice, but not as much of a revolutionary as Chris. He is very artistic, intelligent, and sensitive, but he is critical sometimes.*

*Josh is such a fake. He is so plastic it kills me. We are talking about religion, all different kinds, and whenever Chris and Nick disagree with Mother, Josh says right after them, "Oh God, Mother," and he doesn't know anything about any religion.*

*Rob I don't know very well because I don't see him much, so I might not be accurate. He is very nice and never mean to me, but he gets mad quite easily.*

*Now I will evaluate myself. I am not pledged to the revolution like Chris; I am more like Nick, I think. I don't believe in violence, but I do think we need a change and I am going to contribute with literature. I read everything. Abbie Hoffman, Eldridge Cleaver, Thoreau, Emerson, classics, fairytales, fantasies and ecology. I like nature, and when I get older I would like to live in a commune. I love animals, domestic and wild. I also love music, and my favorite composers are Mozart, Ravel, Berlioz, Debussy, and Chopin. I love playing the piano, but I think I'd like to be a professional violinist.*

In early July, when our lease was up, we moved from the house in Senlis to the Sologne, a wilder area in the Loire Valley.

Cecily's diary from La-Ferté-Saint-Cyr, July 8, 1970:

*I am keeping my diet pretty well. I now weigh 115 pounds. Yesterday I didn't eat the chocolate mousse for dessert and almost died.*

*My four wishes today are:*

1. *I wish I could speak French perfectly.*
2. *I wish I could get a letter from every one of my Lawrence friends within the next two days.*
3. *I wish I could keep my diet.*
4. *I wish Nu-Dang would always be happy.*

*Yesterday we saw the Chateau of Chaumont, which overlooks the Loire River. There is a beautiful park with bridges and a staircase in a tree and stables with gold fittings for the royal horses. Now I'll tell you about Catherine de Medici who lived at Chaumont.*

*Louis XII, he was married to this Catherine, but he loved Diane de Poitiers better and then he died. Then Catherine, who was very mean, traded Chaumont for Diane's chateau, which was more beautiful. It's called Chenonceaux and we're going to see it tomorrow. Then Diane got sad and bopped off somewhere to die. Catherine, you see, was really freaky. She and this astrologer stayed up on top of a tower in the palace studying the stars. So one day this lady decided to read the future of one of her sons. It said he was going to die violently and so she freaked out.*

*In five days we're going to Paris and stay at the Buells for the Bastille Day parade. I'm really excited. What will I wear? I look fat and awful in everything. We may see President de Gaulle; Cousin Bill gets good seats on the parade route because he works at the American Embassy.*

My journal from La-Ferté-Saint-Cyr, July 20, 1970:

*From a previous visit to Europe with the two older children, a new word has entered our vocabulary: Fenouillard. It had come from a movie we had seen in Cannes about the confusion and problems in a French family with many children who traveled a great deal. Since then, any moment of disarray or abrasiveness in our family is called a fenouillard. Well, traveling anywhere can be abrasive, even without children, but this is about a particularly fenouillard day: July 13, when five children, a mother, a father, and an unforeseen complication in the shape of a baby hedgehog were getting ready to leave for Paris in a very small car. We were heading for the last train that day from Beaugency, a beautiful medieval town in the banks of the Loire, and our nearest railroad terminal. We were already late when the overstuffed Peugeot, looking like one of those bulging circus cars, began to move slowly down the drive. Then Roz squeals from the back, "Wait for Cecily! She's not here!"*

*Then, there was Cecily at the car door with that Florence Nightingale look, holding onto a very big box. Charles (in his most cold and austere voice): "WHAT is that?"*

*"It's Herisson," Cecily answers with an ice-melting smile. "Hedgehog, Dad, you know… Roz found it abandoned in*

*the woods. He's hurt, but if he doesn't go to Paris he'll die. Please, Dad, he won't be any trouble."*

*There wasn't time for rationalizations, only expletives from Charles and groans from the other children as the door opens, and Cecily and a large box squeeze in.*

*Out on the main road heading to Beaugency, Chris says from the back, "Dad, I forgot my shoes."*

*From the front: "What's wrong with the ones you're wearing?"*

*From the back: "I'm not wearing any."*

*Groans, more expletives, louder this time. Car stops, door opens, and Chris is told he can't come to Paris for the Bastille Day parade.*

*Arrive at the station—train just pulling in. Charles still suffering from Fenouillard-ism buys one too many tickets. Finds unoccupied compartment on train, sits there defusing. Nick, Cecily, and the twins sit in a nearby compartment with two French women who look perplexed as Cecily starts feeding the hedgehog with an eyedropper. I was just glad she'd had her tetanus booster.*

*The Buell's house is out near the Bois, large and airy Beaux-Arts design. Children milling around everywhere, a goddaughter, lots of cousins. The adult Buells take news of sickly-prickly houseguest calmly.*

*The parade was all that a parade should be, a pageant extraordinaire, and the children did get a glimpse of President de Gaulle.*

*On the night before our departure, the maid discovers Herisson being washed by Cecily in the guest bathroom, which she had just neatened for the arrival of an important dignitary. It was very upsetting to the maid, also to the hedgehog, for he died a few hours later. Burial took place under a flowering almond tree in a Paris garden. All the young attended. Cecily took the loss philosophically, and as for the dignitary, if he found a great many bristles and bugs in his bath, I never heard about it.*

It had always been easy to talk to Cecily about anything. Her curiosity was all encompassing. But it was hard for me to talk to her about sexuality and her changing body. When I brought up a sensitive topic like menstruation, she would say something like, "Mum, I know all that stuff. The school nurse gives us talks and shows us movies." Then she would quickly leave the room.

One day, I got a book out of the library called *Love and Sex in Plain Language* and left it by her bed. With her passion for books, I hoped she would at least look at it. But she ignored the book, and she skipped sex-education classes at school. So she was left with only a rudimentary idea of what was happening inside her body. I learned, much later, that this is part of the anorexic syndrome—the borderline anorexic resists learning about sex, her changing body, hormonal surges, and the turmoil within.

Once she reached adolescence, Cecily came face-to-face with her social inadequacies and sexual immaturity. To all outward appearances, she seemed to have survived childhood happily, but she didn't talk with me or anyone else about her anxiety and episodic depressions. Her period began four months before her fourteenth birthday. She began to see her body as a source of danger, but kept her fears hidden under a mask that she rarely let slip. We, her parents, saw a girl looking forward to wearing uniforms, making new friends at her new school, and riding horseback through the green fields.

All of our children had been baptized and confirmed in the Episcopal Church. They all attended Sunday school, but as teenagers their independent rumblings grew. Roz wanted to go to the Unitarian fellowship because they talked about "interesting" things; according to Chris, it was sex and drugs. According to Cecily, it was because all Roz's friends wore jeans to church.

Now our eldest daughter was on her way to a church school. We just hoped that the religious foundation laid down in her early years would be firm enough for her to build on. At least, she was going to be in a safe environment far removed from the dating pressures of an urban high school. Sadly, we did not see that what Cecily really needed was more time to form her sexual identity and build her self-esteem.

Over that summer, Cecily lost weight. She had reached her full height—close to five feet five—when she left for boarding school that September. She was thirteen years eight months old, and she weighed 108 pounds. She looked healthy.

At first, she wrote cheerful letters home full of news about her new friends and teachers. Homesickness, shadowy from the start, darkened in the winter term. She worried a great deal about Nu-Dang. She had a few close friends, adored her horse, and hated her piano teacher.

Cecily's diary, February 10, 1971:

> *I rode Montana today, and I love him. I am so mad at myself for ever saying anything or thinking anything bad about D. I really love her, and I think I must have been taking out my hate of myself on her. All I've eaten today is a little corn pudding. I still have to start my homework. I was depressed this morning and still am, a little.*

She liked English, especially creative writing. Her story below, entitled "Pop," was chosen to be in the school magazine, *The Steward.*

*Once upon a time there was a beautiful bubble with many windows and doors. It reflected everything in many beautiful colors. This bubble was a very special bubble, because it lasted for a minute, instead of a fraction of a second.*

*It so happened that I fell in love with this bubble, and it was bouncing around my room picking up dust particles. The sun made a beautiful ring of rays around it, and all of a sudden—I'm not sure whether the bubble grew or shrank—everything looked round, curvy, and billowy.*

*I stretched my hand out and it touched something foamy and resilient, but soft and smooth like velvet. I smelled unusually soapy and clean. I was in the bubble. But so were some other people. I asked them who they were and they said, "We are the bubble people. Welcome to our bubble. Come on, it's time to eat." I always wondered what bubble people ate and now I found out. Soap—but it tasted good and bubbly and warm, more like soup. But the minute you swallowed it, you could bounce in the air, rise, and talk about sweet bubbly things.*

*Everybody was clean and sweet, including me. A little bubble path—is that what I saw? Where did it go? I ventured towards it. "No, no, go away!" From nowhere, a million bubble people appeared and crowded and pushed me.*

*"No, you may not walk that path—that is the path of infinity, the bubble's immortality path. You are a mortal. We dreamed you up, and you are not real—this path is only for the real, truly beautiful things. Only we are immortal. You think we last for a second—but do we? No, we are forever*

*drifting and bubbling, invisible to the human eye except at birth. When we pop we are only escaping our dream and progressing towards reality. You have to go now; it's time for the pop."*

*Pop.*

*Now I am sitting on the floor again. My fingernails are dirty, and my hair is greasy. The bubble can is sitting next to me, but my bubble has popped. It's time for me to take a bubble bath. But why does it matter? I am only a dream. I am only a dream.*

Before Christmas, the school nurse wrote us about Cecily's eating "one piece of chicken today and unable to attend class due to fatigue."

Over the holidays, we were uneasy. She had lost only two pounds since September. When she was home for Christmas, she ate. She was polite but quieter. She spent a lot of time in her room rather than getting together with friends or joining in family activities.

The school kept a close watch on Cecily's weight for the rest of the year. She gained fifteen pounds in five months, and, by the end of the academic year, she weighed 121 pounds. But for the first time she was also getting bad grades, and there were shifts in moods and friendships and hints of marijuana.

Then a blow came from an unexpected quarter. Nick, who was in the eleventh grade at Brooks School, took an overdose of barbiturates and wound up at McLean Hospital. After a brief stay in the hospital, Nick finished school at Windsor Mountain and then joined his brother Rob in Los Angeles, where his depression lifted and he began working as a machinist for an inventor.

In late February, Nu-Dang got an infection and died. I decided to tell Cecily about it when she came home for Easter. I put the cat in a box in the garage—the coldest room in the house.

Cecily's diary, March 2, 1971:

*Skipped modern dance this morning but practiced the piano instead—a new beautiful piece by Mozart called Turkish March. Can't wait until Aspen...only 21 more days. Mrs. K [a teacher] is such a snoop and looks more like a varicose balloon each day. Still, it's getting better here. Played tennis with F. and S. and at supper started my new vegetarian diet. Walked to the harpsichord recital in the chapel with B. It was all starry overhead, and we had a good talk.*

I picked Cecily up at the Kansas City airport and told her about Nu-Dang.

"No, please," she cried. "He can't be dead."

Cecily's diary, March 19, 1971:

*I'm home for Easter vacation, but I'm really sad. Nu-Dang died. I think Mother knows how upset I am, but Nu-Dang was like a best friend. I loved him so much, more than anybody will ever know. The house seems so empty. I keep expecting Nu-Dang to walk in, jump on my lap and purr. My eyes are red from crying. I always thought he was immortal. I can't believe this because I was so happy these last weeks at school and all today on the plane flying back from Baltimore. I already miss my friends. Mother is nice... I love her, and Roz is such a freak but I love her too. But I don't think I'll ever stop crying.*

Then a letter arrived from the headmistress of Cecily's School:

*Dear Professor and Mrs. Warner,*

*I have had a long conversation with Cecily and find some of her uncertainties beginning to diminish. She isn't really able to articulate specifics about "what she doesn't like," and I know she is coming to enjoy her life here in several ways. It is apparent to most of the adults that she can indeed handle the work once she "grows up." And that is just it; we feel that another school would present exactly the same frustration to her, and she would be best advised to spend another year here. Therefore, the best professional advice I could give you would be to encourage her to return next fall, knowing the challenge we face and the intelligence that lurks just beneath the surface of this childlike candor.*

We (and the school nurse) failed to recognize that Cecily's difficulties with peer relationships, eating, and schoolwork were deeper and more complex than just "growing up."

Years later, I pieced together how my daughter's poor self-image and preoccupation with body image set the stage for her eventual eating disorder. I am chastened by my failure to see the deeper problems earlier and to seek psychiatric counseling for her.

By summer, Cecily had regained her lost weight but not her self-esteem. The school nurse told us that she was eating better and we hoped two months on the Vineyard would bring back the round cheeks and sunny disposition.

I loved the shape of our Vineyard summers, wide-open spaces ruled by whim and weather. The days always had a timeless quality. Picnics on South Beach, Cecily as a child with a bucket full of sun-bleached shells, kite flying over the dunes, sailing, clamming in the lagoon, peeling noses.

*Pax and I in Lawrence, Kansas*

I still remember the headiness of my first kiss at fourteen years old behind a hedge on North Water Street in Edgartown. Vineyard summers were fixtures in my life. I loved the salt-tasting, drifting days. In summer, the children were in charge of their own days, and I could do what I wanted—sit on Wasque Beach and watch Lesser Yellowlegs skitter along the sand or start a sketch and never finish it.

But there were changes that summer of 1971. Cecily arrived home from school with a rash, looking pale and tired. The doctors suspected mono, but the rash faded with medication. The color in her cheeks came back, but her effervescence was gone. She would spend days by herself and then return in a rush to riding horseback and swimming in the surf.

We thought her shifts in mood were adolescent angst. We had seen enough of that with our older boys. But Cecily's isolation was deeper. The look on her face made you feel that an impenetrable curtain had dropped. It was hard to intrude on her space.

In July, two friends from her boarding school visited us. The girls did all the usual summertime things during the day, and, at night, they slept together in a small cabin behind the tennis court. On the edge of sleep, I would hear their laughter mixed with the sounds from boats in the harbor.

In mid-August, Cecily had to decide whether or not to return to St. Timothy's. We talked about it often during the summer.

She met with the family pediatrician several times that summer, who probably didn't get the full story from the patient. Our doctor never diagnosed her eating disorder or the need for psychiatric intervention. On the question of returning to school, she said, "It should be Cecily's choice. Her weight and blood levels are fine."

Most troubling of all to me is that I didn't even question the pediatrician's advice. Most doctors had never seen an anorexic or bulimic yet. The media never mentioned the subject. Most families didn't know the name of the disorder they were looking at. So everybody missed the danger signs.

"I want to go back," Cecily told us. "I can avoid what I don't like, and there's a lot that I do love—my writing, horseback riding, and friends. It's easier to get close to people at school." We still didn't see the troubled child beneath the sunburn and freckles, so we went along with her decision. She returned to St. Timothy's, tan, healthy-looking, and weighing 122 pounds.

Once at school, she started dieting again. We didn't get letters as often. When we did, she didn't mention her friends as much. This was the first sign that Cecily was withdrawing socially. Her withdrawal intensified as the disease took hold. She saw the school doctor and nurse several times during the year. She felt tired and weak, symptoms stemming from weight loss and the drugs she later admitted taking.

On April 25, 1972, she saw a doctor in Baltimore for nausea and fatigue. Her weight: ninety-five pounds. Her blood tests were normal and diabetes was ruled out.

The headmistress wrote us in the spring about changes in her condition:

*I also realize I've had no chance to pursue with you my concern over Cecily's physical appearance this past term. The sunken eyes and generally tired feeling could never be attributed to any specific illness, and I am still concerned with her overall well-being. Certainly her subdued manner this year is in direct contrast to the effervescence of last year, yet it may just be a sign of growing maturity.*

And in June, she wrote a final letter:

*Although Cecily does continue to baffle many of us—and you, too, I gather—the lengthy exchange we had when you visited this spring has been immensely helpful to me and her teachers. There have certainly been strong areas of improvement in English and French; yet the worrisome side of her weight problem persists in fluctuating. In my own way, I can't help but think the crux of some of this lies in that direction. At a school horse show this spring, I found myself marveling that she—frail as she appears—could still maneuver her mount.*

At least at St. Timothy's she had medical supervision and two years of friendships to lean on. The world of mental illness was foreign to Charles and me. We realized that Cecily needed professional help, but we still felt St. Timothy's was the best place for her.

In hindsight, I still ask myself how I missed the early warning signs. Her anger was increasingly directed at me. Was my daughter the consummate actress? Or was I especially myopic? I couldn't make the pieces fit.

*Rear view of our house on Sandy Pond in Lincoln, Massachusetts*

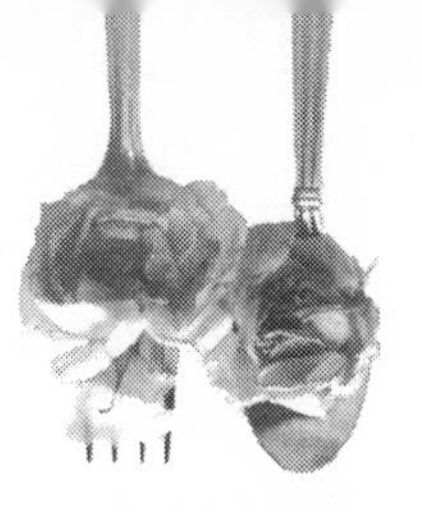

# chapter six

After six years in the Midwest, we moved back east in 1972, into a rambling wood-framed house in Lincoln, Massachusetts. Our house had wide porches and a sweeping view of a large body of water called Sandy Pond. The place was very beautiful—the house, the land, and the pond.

Charles and I were happy to be back on the East Coast, but the older children saw it differently.

"Where do teenagers hang out?" Chris asked the day we arrived.

There were no meeting places for older children, no community center. Lincoln is a classic New England town. On our road, each spring a sign appeared warning, "Drive carefully—turtle crossing." Such quaint oddities were lost on our teenagers, including Cecily, who was disconnected and drifting with few reference points and no friends.

One afternoon, Charles tried to get through to her. Who knows what Cecily must have thought when her father walked into her in her bedroom with a large medical book and in the shattered light of late afternoon, placed his hand on hers. I can imagine the blue corded tendons of her hand standing out against the pallor of her waxy skin.

With a great effort to remain steady and unemotional, Charles pitched his voice low. "Cecily, I want to read you something from this medical dictionary."

Her face was turned away from him and buried in her pillow.

He began reading. "The term anorexia nervosa properly defines the clinical state resulting from psychogenic aversion to food, and consequent emaciation.[2] The—"

"What is 'psychogenic'?" she interrupted.

"It begins in the mind," he answered. "There is no organic base for it."

She pulled her hand away, and he knew he'd lost her.

The telephone had become her enemy. I could see the pain on Cecily's face when the ring was answered and it was for someone else. Frequently, I took the receiver off the hook, and it would stay that way for hours, until Roz arrived home from school. Then the evening hours would be full of other people's plans, other people's laughter. Why couldn't it be for Cecily—someone from Kansas, from Cambridge, from St. Timothy's?

As Cecily's weight kept dropping, her behavior became more unpredictable. This was the start of a new and alarming phase. Her periods of hyperactivity and withdrawal were more marked. After days of eating very little, she would lose her self-control and sneak into the kitchen and stuff herself with butter, honey, cake, cocoa, and quarts of ice cream. Then she would steal away to a remote corner of the house and throw it all up.

We had a man from the hardware store come and put locks on the pantry and kitchen doors. It was a horrible way to live and the other children hated it. In the past, they would have yelled at Cecily, but everyone was quieter now. Doors were closed and behind them whispers.

I found Dr. A, a family therapist, but the sessions didn't start well. Cecily didn't like him and didn't see anything wrong with her weight. She just wished everyone would stop interfering in her life.

Dr. A came up with a plan, the Saturday lunch. We were all to eat exactly what Cecily did. I would place the food in serving dishes on the buffet, and Cecily would help herself. If she took a spoonful of minced chicken and five string beans, we did the same. It was a disaster for everyone, except Cecily, who nibbled at her mouse-sized portions, seemingly oblivious to the feelings of others around her.

Dr. A obviously hoped to shame her into eating more, but his approach only caused eruptions of family rage. Charles had to suffer through back-and-forth drives from Brandeis University where he was teaching a course on Napoleon. How to concentrate on ancient French disharmonies when the power struggle at home was so intense?

Our household was centered on Cecily. The rest of the family was largely overlooked. The other children were baffled. For them, it was a big leap to imagine not wanting to eat. Their patience frayed. On weekends, they all made plans to be somewhere else. Charles felt Cecily was simply being stubborn. He told me on several occasions, "Maybe if you blew up at her sometimes, it might clear the air."

How could I blow up at a shadow?

One night after another exhausting day, the telephone rang. I was already in bed.

Charles answered. I heard him say, "Oh hi, Rob...hanging

in there... What? We told you before. She needs to be under constant surveillance. Yes, both shrink and GP.[3] No, I don't think I'm being uptight. Mum isn't either. Cecily is sick and warm climate has nothing to do with it."

When Charles came to bed, he looked drained. "Dammit, I wish he'd back us up and tell Cecily we're doing the best we can."

"Was there anything he had in mind?"

"The usual bit. If Cecily were in L.A. with him all her problems would vanish into that pure Los Angeles air."

We had spoken often of a setting for Cecily removed from her overinvolved parents. We just couldn't see that her brother's home on the other side of the county was a solution. He adored his half sister and wanted the best for her, but he understood even less than we did about her needs.

"She'd feel marooned in that tiny house wedged between freeways with no way to get around on her own," Charles concluded. "She'd feel even more helpless and watched over than she does here."

A week later, Cecily took some uncashed traveler's checks from her desk and flew to Los Angeles. We phoned Dr. A, who said she must return home immediately. In two days Cecily was back, upset by the fuss and about having to leave her brother.

I put a small begonia plant by her bed with a note saying: *Glad you're home, darling.* I wished Dr. A would share his concerns about Cecily more openly. Instead, he talked about boundaries, shifting alliances, and unarticulated feelings. It was all so puzzling.

A short while after her return, Dr. Gordon Winchell, our family doctor, suggested hospitalization. Cecily's daily caloric intake hovered around 600. Her weight was in the high seventies.

For a week, she was on Emerson Hospital's pediatric unit. Five weeks later, she was back in the hospital, this time on the psychiatric hall.

One night, when the telephone rang, it was for her. It was Michelle, a friend from school, small-boned, ethereal Michelle. Michelle was coming to stay for a while. Something close to hope appeared again in our beleaguered household. Everything was going to be all right.

Two days later, we drove to Logan Airport to pick up Michelle. The girls chatted away in the back of my rattling Volvo all the way home. My spirits were up for the first time in months.

That evening, Cecily came down to dinner, subdued. She joined in the conversation and ate some spoonfuls of chicken and rice pilaf. I told Michelle I needed to talk to her alone. When Cecily had fallen asleep, Michelle joined us in the kitchen.

We told her of our concerns: "We love her so much," I said, "but she's not getting any better. Sometimes a complete change of scene turns the situation around, someone different in charge." We told Michelle about an aunt and uncle in Washington who had offered their home as an alternative. They had five children, and Cecily liked them all.

"That sounds great," Michelle said, "and I'll be close by to help out on the social end."

"She has a job waiting for her at the National Audubon Headquarters and her uncle is looking for a therapist," I said. "There are still a few wrinkles to be ironed out, so don't say a word to her yet."

Charles and I fell asleep easily that night despite the cold north wind blowing down the lake and in through the cracks in our old house. Hope and help-at-hand had a tranquilizing effect. For the first time in months, we made love, remembering what it was to sleep without the specter of despair stretched out coldly between us.

The following morning at the breakfast table, I looked up and saw Michelle in the doorway, visibly distraught.

"Cecily's gone," she said.

Cecily had run away before, but this time she left no clues, no note hinting of California. Why did she go when her closest friend had come to visit?

A policeman arrived and took down the information: *white; 5'4 ¾; 16 (looks 12); 78 pounds; brown hair, long and tangled; face, pale and sunken; eyes, light blue-green; jeans and a navy pea coat.* "Do you have a snapshot?"

"No. She never lets us take her picture, not since she's been sick," Charles said. "I think an old one might be…confusing." He trailed off weakly. "It's just that she looks so different now."

"Could she have gone to New York?"

"What do *you* think, Pat?" he asked me in a low, measured tone.

I tried to concentrate. "No," I heard myself say in a small voice I didn't recognize. "She's too timid for a city like New York, unless she has a friend there."

"Would she go to your mother's?"

"I don't think so."

The policeman was listening and writing it all down in a red notebook.

"But if she does, Mother will call us right away."

The policeman told us New York is the hardest place to find runaways. He didn't hold out much hope. So we hired a private detective who had a track record for finding runaways. He traced Cecily as far as Boston, where she was seen by a conductor on an early-morning bus. There the trail ran out. No one remembered a girl of her description at any of the railway terminals.

For the next two days, we telephoned her friends. We looked through her desk for clues. All leads ended in dead ends.

A week later, my mother was alone in her apartment in New York. Her weekly bridge game scheduled for that afternoon had been called off due to snow. The front door bell rang, and she went to open it, expecting Ollie the elevator man with her copy of the *New York Herald-Tribune.* Peering into the dimly lit hallway, she saw a mask-like face grinning with out-of-proportion teeth and blue flaking lips.

A small voice squeaked, "Mootsie, it's me, Cecily."

Mother led her granddaughter, whom she barely recognized, into the apartment. Cecily was dressed in ragged, dirty jeans and an oversized navy pea coat. She coiled in the corner of the white sofa and picked nervously at a torn cuticle, as withdrawn and unaware as if she were a visitor from another planet.

"I need money, Mootsie. I'm at the Y and can't pay my bill."

"The Y? Does your mother know you're in New York?"

"No. Do we have to tell her?"

Cecily sat with her knees pulled up tightly to her chin. Calls were made back and forth, and a rescue plan took shape.

Cecily would stay in Washington with Charles's brother, Willy, and his family. This was to give her time to heal away from her own family.

Charles and I flew to DC to see her. We spoke to her social worker first. I felt adrift and impatient. His office on Fox Hollow Road was formal and stuffy, except for the smell of lilac that wafted in through the window. I felt the desperate need to find a cure before our daughter dissolved before our eyes. I felt that time was running out.

The social worker and the doctor were looking for any breaks in the chain of our family, anything that could be at the root of Cecily's weight-loss obsession. The doctor was particularly fascinated by my husband's relationship with his father. "You really don't know anything about your father's side of the family?"

"Precious little," Charles replied.

"Before your next visit, Professor Warner, I'd like you to do some homework. You say your father's sister is still living? Look her up. Find out all you can about your father and his story. Family feuds don't have to be passed on like family silver, you know."

Personally, I chafed at the questions. *How will aging aunts and family trees save our daughter? Why won't these doctors see our pressing need? A young life is at stake!*

But, as it turns out, feuds do get passed on, along with values and myths. In this sad process, feelings get buried or ignored. I was beginning to understand how family therapy is *supposed to* work. The idea is that patients can let go of their symptoms as other family members unlock from their customary modes of relating to each other. With more space to move around, "blame" gets lifted off the sick member and only then is change for the entire family possible.

Charles and I had first blamed each other. Then we blamed the media, the movies, the fashion magazines. It hurt too much to look inside, and we didn't even know what we were looking for. Was Cecily, the sensitive child, the symptom bearer for the entire family? Was she the finger pointer to problems in the marriage? I didn't have the answers. But I did know how different Charles and I were from each other. Was that puzzling for the children? It was the same question we had heard from Dr. A, but I was paying closer attention now. But how to sort it out? And was there time left to save Cecily?

Katto, my sister-in-law, had dinner at the same time each night with the help of a cook. We hoped that, with regular mealtimes, Cecily would have an easier time with her eating.

Some evenings, Cecily would eat in the kitchen and not speak at all. Other times, she would join the family in the dining room, eat a little bit, and laugh as Uncle Willy launched into a graphic description of the Atlantic blue crab from his book *Beautiful Swimmers*, which would soon earn him a Pulitzer Prize.

Cecily was eating enough to maintain her weight in the low nineties. She liked her job at the Audubon and got to know her way around Washington. She went shopping with her cousins in Georgetown boutiques. I hoped the new clothes would lift her self-esteem.

One day, Cecily took a train to Baltimore, then a taxi for fifteen miles to her former school, St. Timothy's. Faculty and students were horrified by her appearance and she was sent back to Washington that night in the charge of the school nurse. The episode was a shock for Cecily. She went to a drugstore the next day and bought a bottle of No-Doz, then took most of the pills before Katto found her slumped on the bed. She was rushed to a hospital emergency room, where her stomach was pumped.

That ended the Washington experiment. In early April 1973, she was back home with us on Sandy Pond. She moved from her cheerful, sunny second-floor bedroom to a room on the top floor. Her old room was stuffed with animals, favorite records and books, a bright yellow beanbag chair, and a large nineteenth-century map of Paris.

In contrast, the attic room was small and gray with sloping walls and a narrow north window obscured by a badly cracked shade. I had used the space as a storage area for unused and broken things. In her new room, Cecily placed her sleeping bag on a spare mattress. Around it, she arranged a few possessions—several books, a shoebox with recipes, and a pad of writing paper.

I stopped trying to lure her downstairs and instead climbed up the stairs to her. I was desperately trying to hold onto a daughter who was slipping into her private world. I would leave a meal tray outside her closed door, sometimes with a note: *Let me know about foods that might appeal to you or when you feel like talking.* Once, I left Robert Frost's poem "The Runaway" on her tray. I thought she might identify with the poem's Morgan colt and its fear of being lost and alone.

By early June, the temperature in the attic heated up, and Cecily returned to her old bedroom. She even joined the family for meals, intermittently.

*Thank God, June is over, and Cecily seems less depressed. She still eats pathetically little, but I suppose that's an improvement on the gorging. I can be sure of nothing these days.*

*Yesterday, she came out into the garden where I was weeding and suggested a visit to the Museum of Fine Arts in Boston. No one else wanted to come, so off we went, with a plan to concentrate on the Impressionist period.*

*On this particular day, it hurt too much to look at Renoir's Girls Picking Flowers in a Meadow. One looked like the young Cecily, her eyes mirroring concentration, the body soft, curving, and radiating good health and sunshine. This time I focused on the less emotional still-life paintings and landscapes. Monet's Field of Poppies near Giverny was one we returned to several times that day.*

—My Journal, July 15, 1973

"Do you remember, Mum, when we drove to Chenonceaux and we passed a poppy field and you said, 'Look, it must be Monet's?'"

"Yes, and Dad stopped, and you sat in the middle of the poppies, looking just as if the artist had painted you there."

How bittersweet simple memories had become.

Cecily's roller coaster mood swings leveled off in the summer of 1973. She began leaving the house and walking to the Old Town Hall to pick up the mail with our Golden Retriever, Bilbo Baggins. She would often return with news about a friend of mine she had run into at the post office.

One day her news was extraordinary. She had been chosen to play the role of Laura, the shy, fragile daughter in *The Glass Menagerie* by Tennessee Williams. None of us knew she had even tried out for the part. My reaction was to say no. How could she possibly play the role of someone so like herself? Then, as she began learning her lines, I saw glimpses of the very young Cecily returning—the *can-do* spirit she had showed during music recitals and horseback rides.

The play was performed in the amphitheater at the deCordova Sculpture Park and Museum, which abutted our property. The applause after the performance was long and heartfelt, especially from those of us who knew the ingénue's real-life story.

I was considering homeschooling Cecily that fall when, one day, a brochure from a local school arrived in our mailbox. After reading about its academic program, Cecily showed immediate interest.

"It sounds a lot like Shady Hill," she said. "Can you set up an interview?"

The depression that I feared might follow the theatrical high never materialized. So we enrolled Cecily in the Cambridge School of Weston. It certainly felt wiser than homeschooling by her mother.

Cecily had been at her new school for two weeks when we noticed a lightening in her mood. She walked all the way home one afternoon, a seven-mile stretch, and on arriving home, chattered away enthusiastically about her new roommate, teachers, and courses.

That fall, Dr. T of Boston's Children's Hospital, a female psychiatrist in the slowly evolving field of eating disorders, became interested in Cecily's case. Cecily seemed to like her and we hoped that trust would follow. At long last, we had a firm diagnosis—two, in fact: anorexia nervosa and clinical depression. Years later, I wondered why Dr. T did not recommend hospitalization for Cecily at Children's and wondered why I didn't ask her about it.

The human psyche has many safety mechanisms. Once we accepted that Cecily was sick and that treatment would be difficult, we gradually adjusted to the new reality. At least the nightmare of having to eat what Cecily ate was behind us. That didn't work, which is always the best reason to make changes to an eating disorder program.

With Cecily regularly seeing a psychiatrist and on monitored medication, we stopped living on vain hopes. We stopped saying to friends, "She's coming along" or "Her weight is up." We stopped making social commitments. I rarely left the house unless Cecily left with me.

When I reflect back on those time, I see the bad and the good. I see flashes of my daughter returning to former enthusiasms—Renoir and Mozart, and beaches and fields, and *The Chronicles of Narnia*. There were so many scattered moments of hope that none of us was prepared for her next anguished gesture.

My mother fell and broke her hip in September, so I had to leave suddenly for New York. Before taking off, I talked over a plan with Cecily. "I'll be in the hospital with Mootsie for the weekend, and Dad and the kids will be at your cousin's wedding." Before leaving, I reminded her to telephone Dr. T if she needed to—any hour, day or night.

"Mum, I'll be fine," she said. "I've got a lot of school work to do over the weekend. Don't worry. Give my love to Mootsie." It was a relaxed conversation, but I was uneasy.

Charles and the children returned home on Sunday just before midnight. The house lights seeped through the leaves of the copper beech. Then they noticed Cecily's bike lying semi-hidden in the rhododendron. The kitchen icebox was open. Food was strewn over the tiled counters and tabletops. A large jar of honey was tipped on one side, its contents dripping down the outside of the cabinet.

Charles phoned the police, then grabbed a flashlight and ran to the edge of the pond. Chris and Nick searched the house, cellar to attic. Nick searched the carriage house with its empty dark spaces upstairs once used for hay. Police lights flashed in the driveway. Roz sat at the kitchen table, sobbing.

Nick found his sister lying on a discarded mattress in an empty raftered room in the carriage house. Her neck was cut and blood smeared. She was moaning softly. The firemen and police, visibly shaken, moved quickly. Within minutes, Cecily was on a stretcher en route to Emerson Hospital, sirens screaming in the starless night.

It was a very close call. After this, the doctors made it clear that there was only one course of action: a long-term stay in a psychiatric hospital. We had no choice but involuntary commitment for Cecily. We, her parents, had failed her, and now an impersonal institution staffed by strangers would take over.

Cecily entered the Codman House unit at McLean Hospital on September 22, 1973.

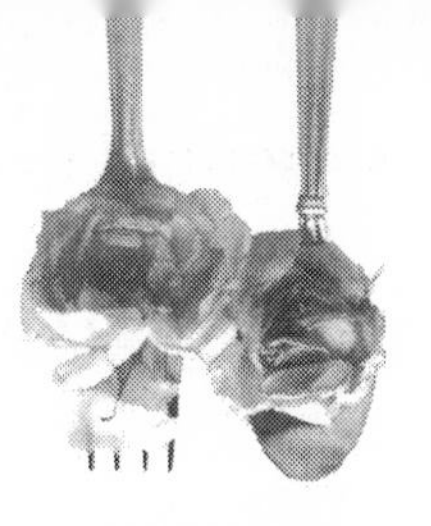

# chapter seven

Since anorexia nervosa was first diagnosed in 1868 by two different doctors—Charles Lasegue in France and Sir William Gull in England—the confusion in the literature swirling around the definition, cause, and treatment of the disease has been considerable. Historically, it was mistaken for tuberculosis and other systemic disorders, as well as endocrine diseases. The therapeutic treatment over the years was equally bewildering: forced feedings, bed rest, intravenous sodium chloride, hormonal infusions, electroshock, insulin therapy, and hypnosis. The variety of treatment methods points to the puzzling nature of this once-rare disease.

Some doctors see it as a specific syndrome, while others fail to differentiate it from other forms of psychologically precipitated emaciation. Therein lies much of the confusion. One thing is certain—a clear diagnosis is necessary to understand the complexities beneath the façade of the perfection-seeking individual who becomes a victim. Once a diagnosis is established, there can be meaningful therapeutic intervention. Just how meaningful depends on so many variables.

Most doctors in the seventies agreed that anorexia nervosa has psychological origins, but that was practically the only area of consensus. As its onset frequently coincides with the first menstrual period, there were many who believed that dieting was begun out of fear of sexuality and adulthood. As about 20 percent of anorexics developed the disease before their first period, other precipitating factors were noted: a desire to be perfect, fear of fat, and any new experience that appeared challenging.

While classical psychiatrists considered anorexia nervosa an expression of oral dependency or a rejection of sexuality, Dr. Hilde Bruch, an early authority in the field, believed such concepts were outmoded and saw a general psychosexual immaturity interacting with the basic issues of the disease. Thus, she cautioned the individual therapist against exploring specific sexual matters before working on the patient's fragile sense of self-worth and her difficulties with personal relationships. Dr. Bruch saw anorexic patients, in most cases, coming from outwardly stable, achievement-oriented upper middle-class families.

The child, having all she can ask for in the way of educational and material privileges, feels she is not being truly heard and so develops her own way of coping. Aiming for perfection, she tries to please everyone. In the beginning, this accommodation works smoothly, and the parents and other authority figures are unaware of the girl's unspoken emotional needs. With puberty, however, her ego deficiencies begin to surface as she starts looking for any method by which she can take control of her life.

The psychotherapeutic treatment procedures aim at meaningful personality change, as well as weight gain. The best method to achieve this goal spawns many theories and no general consensus. Whichever path is chosen, most clinicians agree that the patient will not resume normal eating patterns unless the treatment focus is on the personality deficits, the inner self, rather than on the problem of food rejection.

Management problems are tremendous because there are few illnesses that produce so many changes both in mind and body and few which comprise so many psychiatric categories, ranging from obsessive preoccupations with losing weight to schizophrenic delusions. All agree that the eating-disordered individual is an extraordinarily difficult and challenging patient.

At the beginning of Cecily's hospitalization, we knew little more than what we read in a short entry in a medical journal. All we were sure of was that outpatient treatment had failed. Now we were faced with what we had all along hoped to avoid: a long-term stay in a psychiatric hospital. We soon learned that Cecily was at the most severe end of the eating-disorder spectrum.

Though Cecily was under medical supervision, she did not get psychological help until almost two years after the onset of her illness. This delay was not unusual. In the 1970s, many female teenagers in America were preoccupied with dieting concerns, and few parents had even heard of anorexia nervosa. Had there been any media coverage, we might have seen how far she had slipped from an adolescent with outwardly normal early developmental patterns into a shaky young woman with poor self-image and a craving to be thin. Sadly, we attributed her symptomatic behaviors to teenage angst for far too long.

Most authorities see the fear of weight gain not as the start but probably as the end of a seriously disturbed psychosexual continuum. When malnutrition is at a dangerous level, the first priority must be weight gain. The patient must be persuaded to take nourishment, hopefully voluntarily, but with aversive treatment as a last resort.

A polyethylene catheter was passed through Cecily's nose into her stomach, and a highly caloric liquid was run in, drip by drip, for hours at a time. She was outraged over this painful feeding method. As long as this coercion persisted, she found it difficult to relate to anyone on the hospital staff. She was not assigned a psychiatrist until two months after admission, thus setting the groundwork early on for major problems. In any case, medical staff was now managing her case. Sometimes removing the family component can make a significant difference. Not in Cecily's case. It slowly unfolded that the way that Cecily had manipulated us at home was simply transferred to a hospital setting.

I saw the fear in her eyes, the folding in of her body when it was time for the feeding tube to be inserted into her nose. The emotional pain was as great as the physical pain. I can still hear the anguished cries coming from her room where two strapping aides were holding her still.

In the use of the nasogastric tube, Dr. Bruch warned of the dangers of behavior modification in the treatment of severely anorexic patients. She wrote movingly of some follow-up studies she did on these patients after their release from a hospital. Feeling tricked into weight gain, all cases showed drastic deterioration, one fatally so. She wrote: "Thus, without psychological support and hope for better self-understanding, this method undermines the last vestiges of self-esteem and destroys the crucial hope of ever achieving autonomy and self-determination."[4]

We learned much later that Cecily's nose cartilage was broken and her septum deviated during one of these sessions. It was one doctor's mocking manner, his attempts at humor while struggling to insert the tube that she couldn't stand. I wondered if a humanist rather than a degree-laden psychiatrist would be a better person to oversee this kind of mental health treatment.

Throughout my adolescence, there were many bad days on Wall Street. I learned that money, even if it was rapidly draining away, called for a sense of stewardship. The outer journey never held any fear for me, and no one then spoke about the internal world. Certainly not my parents, who were born at the far end of the Victorian era.

Little wonder that I couldn't speak to the doctors and therapists at McLean, who had their own tunnel vision zeroed in on the anorexic's mother, her profile resting neatly in their files. It gets back to a problem with communication, something that family therapists have always been clear about. How wonderful to be so clear about anything as equivocal as communication.

Grim as the news was from McLean Hospital, my search for understanding kept me from flying apart. My questions never stopped. *How do other mothers manage?* The only other mother I knew with an anorexic child was as baffled as I was.

During this early stage of hospitalization, with only a mental health aide to help her cope with her feelings of pain and betrayal, Cecily slowly drifted downwards into a terrifying world. On the hall, her medication was frequently changed, but no change was evident in the psychodynamics of her disease. "She must regress more in order to improve," we were told.

The doctor in charge of her hall seemed disinclined toward meetings with parents; such distancing was common on the top level. I found that empathy, when I did encounter it, was among the young hall health aides who did truly seem to care.

For hospital visits, each family member had to arrive at his or her own formula for coping. I went weekly, on a schedule, but due to what seemed like a never-ending crisis situation, times varied. Charles, understanding that the ties of dependency had to be cut, restricted his visits to twice monthly.

Cecily's brothers and sister, on the other hand, visited often. Their feelings were conflicted. Josh's words stayed with me: "Mum, I feel guilty when I don't go, depressed when I do." A McLean aide told Nick, "She feels isolated and alone. Your visits would be good for her, but I don't think you'll see behavior change soon."

Charles and I walked gingerly along parallel tracks, touching less and less. We had little time for ourselves and our needs and had so much to learn. It turned out that the book I needed was called *Surviving an Eating Disorder*,[5] but it was not in bookstores until 1988, years too late for our family.

One thing was clear: Cecily didn't like her middle position in the family, with brothers close in age on one end and twins on the other. Sensing this, I had moved closer to Cecily, but this created a family imbalance.

"What's the difference between the ordinary dieter and the anorexic?" Charles asked me one day. That was the only question I could answer with any assurance.

"The ordinary dieter will start feeling better about herself as soon as she gets down to the desired weight—not so for the anorexic. No matter how low her weight drops, she'll feel depressed—not good enough. So her weight keeps falling, and fears take over."

"Fears of what, exactly?"

"Of losing control, getting fat. The anorexic feels the only thing she can control is what she eats. Cecily at twelve was sort of chubby, remember? Losing weight brought compliments. So the disease gets positive reinforcement before it's ever recognized."

I told my mother how the school nurse had first thought Cecily's weight loss was due to diabetes, mono, or simply issues around growing up. In the seventies, most health professionals had never seen an eating disorder case, so it wasn't surprising that Cecily's early warning signs were missed by the school nurse at St Timothy's, a doctor in Baltimore, and her pediatrician in Boston.

Many afternoons we drove over to the hospital to see Cecily. The conversations were stilted. My mother did her best to remember stories from her early days, but the desolate atmosphere of the Victorian buildings with their locked doors and impenetrable steel screens rubbed off on all of us.

Cecily was quiet and remote, and often refused to see us. Under her pallid, mask-like exterior was a great deal of anger at her father and me for keeping her hospitalized and at the staff for "tricking" her into weight gain. The tube feeding was behind her. Now, with the support of Dr. S, her first and only psychiatrist, she began to express her hurt and rage; articulating her anger rather than acting out by refusing food or not taking her "meds."

Now, life at home was returning to something like normalcy. Locks were off the kitchen door. Laughter and music floated through the rooms again. Friends were coming around. One in particular, our next-door neighbor, Nan Ellis, was always coming up with ways to relieve my sadness: a walk to church over the fields, cross-country skiing along the trails that ribboned through our town, a search for spring warblers at Mt. Auburn Cemetery.

Before McLean, Charles and I had moved cautiously, trying to give Cecily as much control as possible, hoping to avoid mealtime confrontations, while growing increasingly alarmed at the sight of her wasting body. Once hospitalized, the staff felt coerced by Cecily's lack of cooperation into adopting measures of negative reinforcement while she responded by holding on ever more tightly to her sick symptoms. There seemed no way to break this circular wheel of action and response. There was no trust between staff doctors and patient, no mutually agreed-upon contract as basis for compromise.

Anger flourished in this atmosphere. Cecily felt betrayed, tricked into giving up the last shreds of control over her body. Nurses, doctors, aides, and family were all party to this great deception. She was not surrendering without a struggle. She began yanking the tube out of her nose, furiously lashing out at doctors as they battled yet again for dominion over her nasal passage, her stomach, her body. She devised ways of retaliating—throwing up her feedings, refusing to speak, on occasion even escaping the hospital. "Playing games," we were told, was "typically *manipulative* like all anorexics," one of the many labels she would receive over her lengthy institutionalization.

It seemed to me, watching helplessly from the sidelines, that the rigidities of her program and the lack of empathy among her male doctors invited negative behavior. In her ward, there was no opportunity to discuss eating problems with a dietician. "She will eat when she understands her intrapsychic conflicts," we were told.

Months after admission, she began to hear voices. The messages warned her not to listen to the men in white jackets who held so much power. Sometimes the voices were accompanied by visions of a tube snake entering her nose. It was clearly a double bind of horrifying proportions. She was being asked to choose between two equally unacceptable alternatives—to drink high caloric liquid or be force-fed through the nasogastric tube. The impasse resulted in hallucinations. A new diagnosis was added to Cecily's patient file: schizophrenic.

The staff responded with isolation rooms, camisoles used for restraint (like a straitjacket), and stronger medication. She was moved to a hall for patients needing acute care and constant observation.

As months stretched into years, I saw why psychiatry is such a baffling discipline and why the psychological rubrics one finds in medical textbooks often do not fit smoothly when put to use in the field. On the one hand, psychiatry can be viewed as an exact science where children go through clearly defined stages, as described by Sigmund Freud, Erik Erikson, and Jean Piaget. Progress through these stages of human development, whether slow or rapid, is sequentially ordered, each building upon the preceding one, with results tabulated along the way. On the other hand, there are parts as fragile as butterflies' wings—a mix of dreams, wishes, impressions, and feelings. Surely, both halves are necessary to better understand the human condition.

It's no wonder there was confusion among the authorities. There was such a jungle of overlapping theories and so little consensus. At one time, I knew nothing about this field, and now felt buried under an avalanche of disconnected facts: so many claims, so few certainties. The pieces of the puzzle were there, if only I could have fit them together.

I started spending days at the library. I felt I was in a race against time. If only I could read fast enough, become wise enough. In my most depressed periods, I felt helpless, a paralyzed witness to Cecily's lonely battle. In my better days, I felt insight would bring behavioral change and resolution. Should I try to understand what happened to Cecily outside a sociocultural context or solely focus on childhood traumas for causality? After all, each one of us is a mirror reflection of our period in history. It is of no small significance that the three children in our family who suffered most in adolescence were the three middle ones, the children of the sixties. I thought Cecily's innate sensitivity, her middle position in the family, and her body image were a major cause of her disease.

It is possible to believe that Cecily's life might have evolved differently had there been stability and consensus in our home. After three years, Charles and I had worked our way slowly and painfully through the guilt labyrinth and had come to believe in life's imponderables. Though most in the field of psychiatry would give scant support to a hypothesis built around "fate," Dr. Robert Coles is one who did. Recently, I came across this introductory passage to one of his books: "The mind's fate is after all, a person's fate. We are drawn along by our private visions, but beyond them stretch almost to infinity for each of us the vast and compelling mystery of chance and circumstance."[6]

Most psychiatrists avoid speaking about the ironies of life. It takes a special individual with humility and heart. Today, there are a growing number of professionals who believe in multiple causations for eating disorders. Among them, Garfinkel and Garner, who see them as "complex psychobiological phenomena and a clinical entity, the final common pathway of forces as diverse as fashion, social expectations, and delusional belief."[7]

It was in this period that I found a book entitled *The Siege*.[8] The author, Clara Park, was the mother of an autistic child, and she wrote out of anger about psychiatry in America, about the barricades it erects to keep parents at a distance, about its cold professionalism. Clara Park was speaking directly to my ripening rage at being exiled from my daughter's personal battle and to the lack of compassion among her doctors.

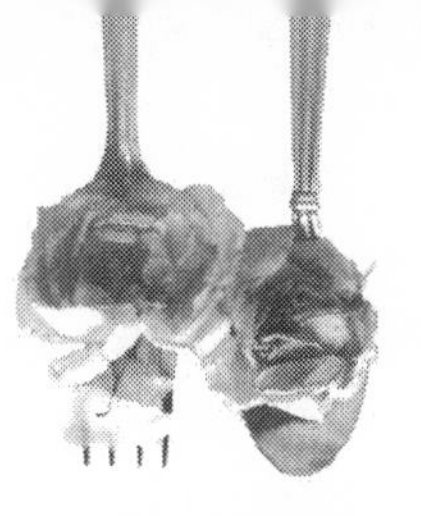

# chapter eight

The autumn of 1974 went by quickly. The mellow light playing on the trees and bushes around our house tinged them in a vague exoticism, like meeting old friends in a foreign country. Or maybe I was just slowly noticing things again and letting myself feel a bit more hopeful about Cecily's recovery. I was enjoying the children I tutored at the Lincoln Elementary School.

Roz was away that year, finishing up at Purnell School, an all-girls boarding school. I missed her enthusiasms and the way her feelings lay close to the surface. I missed our talks and tennis matches. "I love her, Mum," she told me one day, referring to her sister, "but I hate what she's doing to you and Dad and the whole family. We can never have fun anymore. All we ever talk about is anorexia."

Josh was the only child living at home that year. He was attending Middlesex School, which was only eight miles away in Concord. On weekends, the house was alive with rock music and sprawling, sloppy seventeen-year-olds who were undirected but bright. Occasionally, Josh stopped off at the hospital to see Cecily, always bringing along something to please her, sometimes a poem he had written and dedicated to her.

"We have some good talks," Cecily told me.

Josh was getting Bs at school in psychology and had started to feel he had a grip on the frailties of the human condition. That summer he taught tennis to a group of disadvantaged kids from New York. Burgeoning signs of maturity appeared but were hardly consistent. One afternoon, Josh smuggled a few joints into McLean and was caught smoking them in Cecily's room. Summarily ejected from the hall, he was banned from any visits for six weeks. The punishment was particularly hard on Cecily, who had so few visitors and so little connection with the outside world.

One evening, Charles and I renewed a conversation we had started earlier as I wandered around in a slip, leaving a talcum powder trail while deciding what to wear.

"It's what she does with all her relationships," I said.

"What is?" he asked.

"This polarization, seeing people as all good or all bad. I was top god in her mythology, now it's Greg at the hospital."

"So what's the danger there?" Charles interrupted. "He seems very levelheaded."

"Of course he is, but don't you see? There are no in-betweens, no gray areas for her. When he's not perfect, he's the world's meanest social worker."

"How do I look?"

"Fine, fine."

Charles was busy trying to hang a replica of a small bear on his watch chain and was not even looking at me.

We were going to dinner at the Tavern Club, which was first established in 1884. Charles was a member, but it was still a rare occasion. It was only on theatrical evenings that wives and children were allowed in the club.

The scheduled play on this February evening in 1975 was called *All About Maizie.* The author was Thomas Boylston Adams, a Lincoln neighbor of ours and one of the club's wittiest members. He was playing former President of the United States John Adams, his ancestor. It was perfect Hollywood casting, the Puritan Adams playing against Charles, wearing my mother's mink beret, as seventy-year-old Benjamin Franklin, Commissioner to the Court of France, philanderer extraordinaire.

After the performance, Nick told him, "You were great, Dad."

"Best Franklin ever," Chris agreed.

While pulling out of the underground garage, I asked Charles about the commissioners, "Why were they in France anyway?"

"Pat, you know Tavern plays don't have to fill in all the gaps, but…" He paused to maneuver around a large truck, then continued, "France needed allies to back its cause, to pay for the Revolutionary troops, and Lafayette turned into a very good friend."

"Friends, schmends," Roz mused, sleepily. "I remember Cecily making lists of her friends in Kansas."

I wondered if Cecily's focus on friends and their opinions was excessive, maybe an early sign of a fraying sense of self. I thought again about the letter from her fourth-grade teacher at Shady Hill School. *Young for her age group*, she had written. *Cecily's immaturity shows away from the classroom and in her eager desire to please her peers.*

What if I had seen in this brief sentence an early warning sign of danger ahead? What if we had held her back a year? What if? What if?

Winter lasted an eternity that year. Then finally, one morning, Burpee's seed catalog arrived in the mail, and my grievances against the world began to fade as I rifled through colorful pages of flowers for all occasions, shade or sun, sweet soil or acidic, annuals or perennials. And such a litany of graceful names: Glory Hallelujah, Festiva Maxima, Coral Cascade, and Scarlet Pimpernel.

In early March, I heard the brook running again. The geese would be back before the saffron yellow showed in the forsythia bushes beyond the rock garden, before the blue scilla pushed up through the early April lawn. The geese always found a safe route home through bad weather and fair, over rivers and mountains. With dark necks stretched out far beyond their large, grayish bodies, the majestic Canada geese would find their way back again to Sandy Pond.

For many months, it had been impossible for me to concentrate. I was drifting on a current, floating from one rocky encounter to another. Even reading was a chore, but then slowly, as the healing sunlight uncurled itself catlike over the land, I felt I was changing, too. One day I realized I had almost finished *Walden* and was beginning to appreciate Thoreau.

I got deeply depressed whenever I thought about Cecily, but my darkness lifted during walks around Walden Pond and Sandy Pond, which were ideal settings for letting go of tensions, guilt, and fears. I had arrived at a way of coping with the stresses of Cecily's hospitalization.

By my fifty-fourth birthday, Cecily had been in the hospital for two years and eight months. Any hopes for a quick recovery were long gone.

*Arriving at the hospital, I find her crunched under a blanket in the corner of the hall. Joining her on the floor, I take her hand in mine, and soon realizing that she is not going to speak, I begin a story that I remembered her loving from happier days. It is about a bird of the sea and tidal flats, a male barnacle goose from a small island in the Outer Hebrides. I talk about his feelings as alone, storm-racked and afraid; he gets blown off his usual migratory pattern, blown across the Atlantic onto the shores of Labrador. Hoping this favorite story might break through the encircling silence, I talked on very softly, watching for a sign. It felt like hours, when maybe it was only minutes… She does not hear me at all.*

—My Journal, May 18, 1975

I have slowly and painfully come to understand these periods of total withdrawal. She had learned that those who say they love her would only betray her trust and separate from her. In rare good moments, Cecily understood why we had to leave her in the hospital with total strangers. At other moments, she hated us for it, forgetting the many months we battled her disease so ineffectually at home.

She saw her siblings marching on happily in step with their friends, shaping their own lives, while she lived on within hospital walls—watched and weighed, protected and medicated, as slowly pieces of her self crumbled away. She saw some of the staff and patients whom she had grown to like switch halls or leave the hospital. Why couldn't they understand her need of continuing friendships and closeness even as she angrily pushed their overtures aside? She certainly couldn't trust the doctors who showed up in her room with the nasogastric tube.

Better not to trust anyone, she felt. Best to concentrate on the only area where she reigned supreme: starving herself to show that she alone was in charge of her body. That was her triumph, her sense of empowerment. She was too sick for the psychiatric path to wellness. The hospital's focus was on saving her life.

Through the months that stretched into years, I wished I had pushed the idea of family therapy more vigorously before I lost hope in the doctors.

I had come to realize that I was able to reach meaningful resolutions more easily by quieting my voice at home in order to avoid confrontations with Charles.

Cecily was simply the change agent.

*I am spiraling down into sleep, tumbling over and over, suffocating in a maelstrom of clouded memories, warring sounds, and hurts. I reach for the center, something solid to cling to, and just manage a fingernail grip on the edge. Pieces keep sloughing off in my hand, crumbling into dust, and I keep falling. The center, however, is still there, barely holding. How long can I withstand this siege?*

*Swimming up from these dark terrors, I find the bed in shambles, my head pounding inside a helmet of steel. I reach for the pills. Slipping a Cafergot under my tongue, I become slowly aware of the recumbent figure next to me. I am enmeshed in self-pity and aching all over, so why isn't he awake, worrying about my nightmare, my migraine, me?*

*The fear of falling and failing and now the angers are tightening inside me like a silent scream. My anger at Cecily for being so sick, at Charles for withdrawing, anger at my hurt and powerlessness and all the missed warning signs. But my guilt was slowly lifting. I loved Charles and hated to see him depressed but was starting to understand that I couldn't make it right for him until I felt comfortable with myself.*

*Love kept sliding down the cracks, ephemeral as skywriting. Charles, touch me, I'm here, wanting you, I cry out, but he doesn't hear me. He's barely awake, tearing at a new package of Salems, preparing to greet another bummer of a day.*

Soon after her arrival on the acute care unit, Cecily started having seizures. The doctors could find no organic reason for them. Could they be caused by dietary deficiencies or a biochemical imbalance, a genetic factor or a head injury? During force-feedings, Cecily would purposefully bang her head against the wall. What was the connection between these compulsive behaviors, her eating disorder, and blows to her head? Certainly any one of these was a possibility, but it was most likely because she was overloaded with too many prescription drugs.

One morning in April, a psychiatric aide telephoned to say Cecily had run away from the hospital. The pattern had been set, but this time there was a difference. On the way she stopped at a drug store and purchased No-Doz and Sominex. I still get angry when I think of an eighty-four-pound waif being sold such potentially lethal medication. By the time she arrived at home, the damage was done. Staggering up the stairs, she made it to the top, and then collapsed onto her bedroom floor, trapped in a vice of muscular rigidity. Again, she was rescued by Lincoln's fire and police department and sped to Emerson Hospital. The cause of this seizure activity could be guessed at, but the symptoms pointed to epilepsy, an organic brain disorder with no cure.

Dispiriting as this news was, there were areas of hope. Dilantin was controlling the seizure activity. The trauma of the feeding tube was over; it would only be used as a last resort when her weight dropped below eighty pounds.

Since her seventeenth birthday, she had begun to reach out to others and was keeping her weight in the low nineties without the tube. Staff, patients, and family told her how nice it was to see her smiling. She had started mingling in the hall community.

Then, negative reinforcement entered in the form of two spaced-out male patients who made a move on Cecily. She had always guarded her personal space. So it's not surprising that she would be uncomfortable, even fearful, of anyone moving too close. I was told she was too sick for psychotherapy or nutritional counseling.

My anger continued to build; in large part over the program her doctors at McLean had imposed on her—negative reinforcement, the camisoles, the quiet room. "She will eat," one doctor had told us, "when she understands her intrapsychic conflicts."

"Damn psychobabble!" Charles snorted, putting his own spin on the nightmarish situation our daughter faced at the hospital.

Some days, Cecily pushed everyone aside and stayed in her room. She was often writing, filling up pages of loose-leaf notebooks with words that movingly described her own private world:

> *I live in a world of fantasy called the land of Cokagyne. I dream that I am the most beautiful girl in the world and live in a crystal palace. This place is a labyrinth of amusements, riddles, and puzzles, enough to keep a philosopher busy all his life. The elixir of life is carried through the outside air—it is the drink of the palace crowd. Every morning it drifts across the face, waking one with its dew. There is no sickness because there is no desire for sickness. The royal scrolls are*

*kept in an old, musty library. At night the velvet interior is reflected in mirrors by fire and candlelight—there is much singing around the hearth. The odd thing is the priest in the tower. They worship deities called cats. The cats rule supreme in the land. The head cat at my particular palace is a Persian with amber eyes. The gardens are planted under his order, chefs and grooms are there to hunt for his dishes, provide amusement for his moods—ladders, yarn, opium mice, bells, and rubber balls. He had formerly lived in England so he dined on eggs, kippers, cambric tea, and cod-liver oil. He had a glossy silver coat, and his name was Tobias—never "Toby," he wouldn't hear of such a thing. Tobias, since leading the so-called good life, had one small problem; he tended towards embonpoint, which was inexcusable. Now the question was how to diet without insulting the master chef… Whoever can think of an answer to this sphinxian riddle, please reply: Tobias, The Crystal Palace, Land of Cokagyne, No stamp needed (the never-bird will deliver).*

In this period, I understood so little about what was happening. Yet again, the only question I could think to ask was, *How long?*

*Cecily, my twin brother Peter and I*

# chapter nine

My mother, by then eighty-six, arrived with my twin brother, Peter, for a two-month visit during the summer of 1974, the summer of the Watergate trials.

Mother moved with difficulty, with the help of an aluminum walker, but she was always the main attraction in any setting. “Wobbly on my legs, I am,” she would say, her milky-blue eyes coming alive, “but not weak-minded.” Her infirmity clearly bothered her. She knew she had little time left but kept this to herself. There was so much else to talk about.

I left old family scrapbooks and photo albums in her bedroom, which she peered through intently, even with her vision blurred from recent cataract operations. Could she make out two-and-a-half year-old Cecily at the water’s edge trying to catch waves in her bucket? Or Cecily at five standing proudly on her first pair of skis in front of a melted snowman? Or Cecily at eight looking small on top of a large white horse?

Once, upon entering Mother’s bedroom, I heard her murmuring, “Such an affectionate, sunny child, such fun.”

Shortly before Christmas, my mother got pneumonia and was taken to Columbia Presbyterian Medical Center, but she refused to stay for long. "Absolutely not," she told her doctor. "No operation, no cancer talk with my children." She was in charge. She left her room at Harkness Pavilion and returned to her apartment on the Upper East Side.

"A month, at most," the doctor told us. A nurse stayed with her to administer pain medication. Jack, my brother, brought over a Christmas tree. "Put the angel higher," he said. "More tinsel, the star's too perfect, the best tree ever." Children and grandchildren arrived for good-byes and tears.

Writing about her mother, Simone de Beauvoir, a founding voice in the feminist movement, struck a chord in me: "It seems impossible to think of my mother dying, not now, now in the Xmas Season, not ever. For my mother had always been there, and I had never seriously thought that someday I should see her go. Her death, like her birth, had its place in some legendary time."[9]

I left my mother's bedside and flew back to Boston to spend Christmas Eve at McLean with Cecily, who had been on a rampage for the last ten days, stubbornly fighting staff at every turn. Not surprisingly, permission to come home was denied, so we all went to the hospital as a family.

There we found Cecily enveloped in an oversized Viyella shirt, her eyes too muzzy from the Taractin to notice the special Christmas gift Nick brought along for her—his artistic rendering of *Why the Chimes Rang*. Roz put a Strauss waltz on the record player. I remember Charles bowing formally, kicking off his boots, and asking me to dance.

I was having trouble concentrating. Shutting my eyes, I was eighteen again, back in the chandeliered ballroom of the Plaza Hotel in my favorite evening dress with the silver lamé bodice. The white tulle frothed up around me in clouds of spun silver. Memories of Christmases past kept running in my head: trimming the tree with old family ornaments, hanging stockings on the mantel, leaving cookies for Santa. But my thoughts kept returning to my mother dying in her New York apartment.

When the waltz ended, the music was replaced by the sound of rock music bouncing off the walls and echoing through the hospital corridors. I noticed a knot of people in the doorway. Dressed in ragged jeans and a pajama top, Steve, a boy Cecily particularly liked, was smiling tentatively as if trying to recapture an elusive memory, lost like his identity in the chemical mists of McLean.

Roz and Josh were dancing in a cleared-out corner of the cluttered room. Cecily was sitting close to Nick on the floor, hair covering her face so I couldn't see if anything was getting through to her. Charles caught my eye and formed the letter V with his fingers, the old Churchill victory sign.

What did it matter if the Rolling Stones replaced the Messiah and the setting was a mental hospital? We are each one of us alone, each on our unique journey, but we were traveling along the same route, sharing sadness, signs, touching, caring. On the way, childish games turned into cocktail parties and children turned into adults, having absorbed the message that individual fulfillment is a right.

You know you've been there when you look in the mirror late at night with burnt-out eyes are and you know your hurt can't be cured with pills or surgery. You know you have been there when your fiftieth birthday has passed and your mother is dying. You are on your own now. You are the older generation, and those who follow are poised to repeat your mistakes.

Christmas past is Christmas present. Each Christmas rolls into the next—bundling down the years—and time pleats like an accordion.

Cecily's new friend on the unit was Tara, waif-like, another anorexic. Sometimes, Cecily liked her very much, and other times, she disliked her with equal fervor. On good days, they talked about commonalities that linked them, like the need to be in control. On bad days, Cecily saw Tara as a prettier younger girl who weighed less and got the lion's share of attention.

Another hospital friend was Anthony, a blind, black fourteen-year-old, another lost child in our society. He called her "Cecily-de-bones" in a soft, caring voice like a young Ray Charles. He wrote her a card in Braille for her birthday, and she suggested a few small things that I might bring over for him, mostly food. On my desk is a plastic letter holder Anthony made for me. Then one day he was gone, pushed on by the courts and the state to his next way station on a lonely journey of makeshift accommodations and fractured relationships.

Being passive witnesses to so many mood changes in our daughter, Charles and I did not dare get our hopes up. We tried to establish some reference points in our own lives. I needed points that were clearly visible, like the aviary migration each spring back to our thawing corner of the earth. For Charles, it was in the skies, tracking constellations as they wheeled across the heavens, directed by God's order.

Many evenings, Charles did not come to bed until stars had paled in the new morning. Sometimes I'd join him, and sometimes I'd toss restlessly for hours, watching the slivers of moonlight enter through the cracks in the venetian blinds. It was in this suspended state that the brand names of the drugs tried on Cecily would wheel through my brain like a Gilbert and Sullivan patter song: Thorazine, Stelazine, Librium, Dilantin, Taracton, Tegretol, and Haldol. I wondered if anyone had ever returned from such a chemical invasion.

*Charles with his mother, Leonora, and grandmother, Marie*

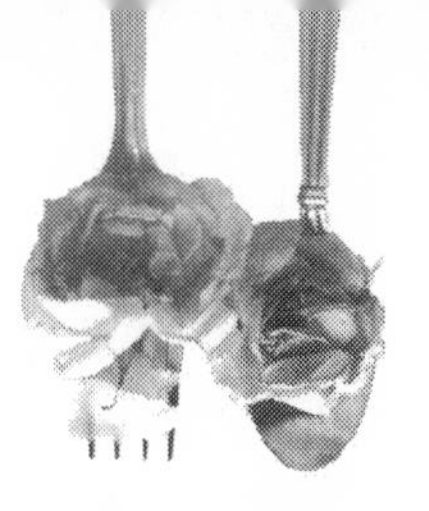

# chapter ten

In my husband's family, it all began with beer. Charles's great-grandfather founded the Haberle Brewing Company in the 1880s in Upstate New York, which jumpstarted the family fortune. The business flourished, and so did the family, but, for the next generation, Syracuse lost its luster. Glamorous and glistening on the horizon of limitless ambition lay the city of New York. Charles's grandmother, Mrs. George Kavanaugh, like Edith Wharton's Leota B. Spragg, was eager to answer the siren call.

Mrs. Kavanaugh and her two daughters, one being Charles's golden-haired mother, Leonora, moved to a townhouse off Fifth Avenue (Belle Époque, of course). The trio moved up in New York cafe society like a flaming troika. There was the townhouse near Central Park, the summer home on the New Jersey shore, the town cars (Hispano-Suiza and Rolls-Royce), first row seats at the Metropolitan Opera, and a table at El Morocco.

This was the world Charles and and his younger brother, Willy, grew up in, which might have been pleasing except for the dark areas that no one spoke of: a father's abandonment and a bitter divorce. It was a world of men's clubs, children's camps, summer resorts, trips to Europe on ocean liners, and money you inherited in trust and left at death for your heirs.

The two brothers attended a private day school in New York City and then St Paul's, a boarding school in New Hampshire, where they both flourished. As they grew older, they drifted into the orbit of their peers whose money was old and carried responsibilities, whose townhouses had libraries with books of oiled, tooled leather.

Their maternal grandfather, Colonel George Washington Kavanaugh—he liked his whole name—was a loud man of small build and firm convictions. The feud was on from the beginning between him and his two grandsons. An outspoken man, the colonel complained that living with two rambunctious boys was not conducive to his serenity.

With time, his language grew saltier. "Your mother runs around with every gigolo in Europe. You boys are bums, just like your father. You'll never rise higher than the source." Willy and Charles knew there was usually no obvious reason behind his anger, so they just tried to stay out of his way.

"Do you think, Mr. Warner, that your mother felt comfortable in the mother role?" (*Comfortable* was one of the therapist's favorite words.)

"Not in the slightest," Charles replied. "She was obsessed by her quest for eternal youth. She went to incredible lengths to cover up the ravages of time—hair dyeing, fake curls, a smorgasbord of diet and health fads. She even subtracted years from her birth date for her passport."

"How do you remember her?"

"Always dressed for a party, always saying good-bye. She was a night person, spent most of the day in bed. I remember the feel of her jewelry, and her perfume smelled like lilies. When I met the mothers of my friends, I realized how flamboyant her lifestyle was—the jewels and furs, the society columns, and parties. I wanted her to be like my friends' mothers, who drove around in ordinary cars and came home at night to ordinary families."

"Did you ever ask her about your father?"

"Of course. Her answer was always the same, 'I never want to hear *that man's* name again!' Friends would ask me, 'Where does your father live?' I'd just laugh. When a form for camp or college required the occupation and address of my father, I left those lines blank. It would have been easier if he were dead. I had fantasies that my father was at all my graduations but then silently slipped away."

"Did you ever meet him?"

"The first time I met him was in Reno when I was five and they were getting divorced. The second time was at my brother Willy's wedding. He was living in a run-down flat on the Upper West Side and saw the wedding announcement in the *Herald-Tribune*. He called to say he was coming. Mother screamed, 'Tell that man he's not invited!' I arranged to meet him at the Plaza Hotel. At the Palm Court, I searched for a familiar face, but how could I recognize a man I hadn't seen since I was five?"

The therapist waited for Charles to finish.

"He finally found me and I told him that my mother didn't want him at the wedding. 'How very unreasonable of Leonora,' he said. I thought I'd solved the problem, but the next day he showed up at the wedding and stood at the back of the church. He came through the reception line at the River Club and my mother didn't even recognize him! Pat went to sit and talk with him. He was transfixed by a tanker moving up the East River.

He said, 'I sailed on one just like that.' He simply wasn't interested in either of his sons."

I knew not having a father in his life affected Charles. We had planned to ask his father to spend Christmas with us on Beacon Hill, but then we learned of his death. Charles's relationship with his absent father was left unresolved.

In spite of his mother's profligate lifestyle, Charles and his brother inherited a comfortable trust. Three generations had been upwardly mobile, but now Charles saw himself leading his family onto the down escalator. To dip into capital was the unpardonable sin in Old Money families. All these withdrawals from capital to pay hospital bills made him feel like a fiduciary failure. Charles feared where it would all end. He was feeling his age.

"There must be some way of getting through to her," he said one day in the social worker's office. "Some way of getting through her anger."

"You sound depressed, Mr. Warner."

"Damn right," he answered bitterly. "She doesn't have a monopoly on depression or anger. All these years I've played by the rules. We had money, but, well, Pat just never wanted to leave the children with babysitters for long and—" He stopped, as if he had forgotten for a moment where he was going with the thought.

"You were talking, Mr. Warner, about playing by the rules," the social worker prompted.

"Yes, I served in the army. I did my duty," Charles went on.

His cigarette had gone out. He stopped talking and relit it from the butt he had left glowing in the ashtray. Two and a half packs a day was his way of dealing with stress. He had repeatedly tried to quit and failed, just as he had with AA. Charles felt trapped in a maze of responsibilities with no clear exit.

The next blow fell in the autumn of 1975 when all part-time faculty members at Brandeis, including Charles, had their appointments terminated. The university had been a steadying anchor and I wondered how it would be having him home all the time. Untenured faculty had become an endangered species. Charles felt on the verge of extinction at fifty-seven.

From then on, his focus was on our money problems. With the financial drain of McLean Hospital, Charles wondered how we could survive if there were another long illness in our family. How much longer could we afford private care for Cecily, and was it fair to the other children? He studied our portfolio and sold off blue-chip stocks in favor of investments promising higher yields. As if things weren't bad enough, Charles got a letter from the IRS that said we were being audited.

The IRS could not believe our astronomical hospital costs. We could not qualify for Medicaid, and our insurance did not cover expenses associated with a preexisting condition. It was so unfair that medical illness was covered while mental disorders were not. Reading the fine print on an umbrella policy we had, Charles discovered a provision that didn't exclude mental illness, even when a suicide attempt was involved. Our policy covered two-thirds of a year's hospitalization.

With that break, we looked at other places to save money. We started selling possessions, the accumulation of things from the past—paintings, silver, jewelry. We didn't need them and would scarcely miss them. The house was something else. Could we really part with our home on Sandy Pond? Could I stand another move? Charles loved the house, especially in its summer face. I loved it in all its moods, even with the wind blowing down the lake in the winter, but it was so costly to maintain.

Since Cecily's hospitalization, I saw dark shadows everywhere and had a recurring full-color dream: a small country village like a Chagall painting with farm animals floating over rooftops, and a frail, dark-haired girl in a white diaphanous dress holding a fiddle. I screamed up at her, "I love you, please come down so we can talk!" But she always floated away higher, until her dress billowed out like a sail and she vanished behind a cloud.

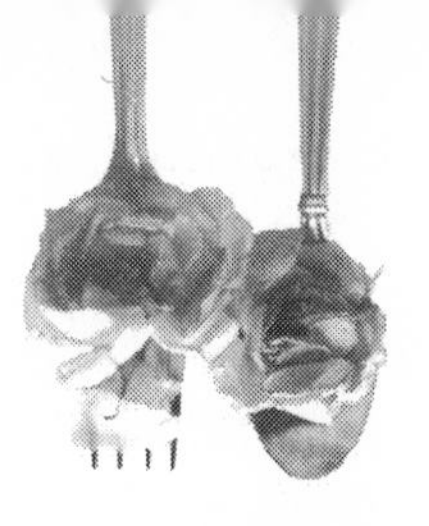

# chapter eleven

It was springtime once again. The land was untidy and winter bruised. It was a time for neatening both outside the house and in, but I could only think of Cecily's piteous plea: "Mother, take me home. I can never get well in this place." With the return of the warm weather, we hoped to see Cecily accept more responsibility and to reach out to a few of the patients on her hospital unit. She did seem to be moving erratically in that direction.

*It is almost our nation's 200th birthday, and there are celebrations going on everywhere. Chris is building a wooden skiff, copied from a 19th century plan right in our front yard, which seems appropriate for this bicentennial spirit. Charles spends much time searching the heavens for a sign of celestial rejoicing, and, praise be, he found it in the form of Epsilon Lyrae, a fine double star 200 light years away.*

*It is mind-boggling to think that the light from this star has been on its way here, traveling through space at a speed, Charles tells me, of 186,000 miles per second. The sky is incredibly beautiful these nights, but the dimensions are so vast that I find it impossible to mold them into my shrunken form of reference. In a few days the Tall Ships are coming to Boston. We are going to move along with them down the harbor on a day liner chartered for the occasion. I am excited.*

—My Journal, July 2, 1976

Charles was spending more and more time at the Tavern Club, lunching with friends, planning evening theatricals, trying not to think of the family dramas and hoping no one will ask. One day, the Tavern Club's 1978 Christmas card arrived in the mail:

*Every twelve months, fixed in its declination*
*A star breaks clouds that hide it from our sight.*
*Providential conjecture, for its light*
*Burning in the emptiness of a longer night*
*Might well suggest what cannot be.*
*Old friends, old songs, old customs, passing, gone.*
*Remembered scenes etched on mind's glass, broken.*
*All our months we know our loss.*
*Bear it, play with it, escape it too*
*In numerous preoccupations, finding mystery*
*Only on the inside of the year. But with friends*
*Mystery holds back shadows, gathering the light*
*In one small hall, well-loved place where Taverners invite*
*Mary, Joseph, and their small child to spend the night.*

"Christmas Poem," by Charles Warner

Writing poetry for Charles was both a comfort and a challenge, but not one he felt he could pursue as a career. "It's beautiful," I told him. I suggested he send it to Frederick Morgan, a good friend who was editor of *The Hudson Review*, but

Charles didn't think it was up to their standard. Years later I used the same poem as the family Christmas card, with insertion of "families" in place of "Taverners," and Nick added a delicate wash drawing.

"Why didn't you tell me you hated moving?" Charles asked me late one winter night. We were talking in the sitting room by the fire with the cold north wind blowing in from the lake. "If you didn't want to move, why didn't you say so at the time?" Charles asked, tight-lipped and unsmiling. He was trying to get my attention by speaking very slowly as if he were teaching English as a second language. "Why didn't you say anything?"

"I guess I thought if the move was right for you, it would be right for the whole family," I told him. I was remembering the look of excitement on his face each time we packed up for another university town.

"If moves are so damaging, why aren't mental hospitals filled with children from the army, theater, foreign service." He paused. "Are you trying to tell me that Cecily is anorexic because of our moves?"

By this time, I felt sure there wasn't a single route to mental breakdown. I said, "The closer I look, the more uncertain I am about everything." He was silent as he stacked dinner plates in a precise manner on the shelf over the kitchen sink. "Then I heard myself saying, "Sometimes I think you'd like to do what your father did."

He stiffened and turned toward me, and said in a steel-edged voice, "What *exactly* do you mean by that?"

"I mean, live in Florida on a boat and follow the sea. No entanglements." It was too late to go back. How did a conversation about our constant moving end up being about his father? Our talks about moving and money rarely ended well—just provoked anger, a reality familiar to parents of a child in therapy.

What Charles wanted was graduate students, less committee work, more specialization, better salary, all rungs on the academic ladder. "Almost every French historian I know has had more time in France than me. Look at the Grants—they have little money, and he's off to La Rochelle in September, plopping the three kids in a lycée. How can I write about France if I never go there?"

I didn't want to move the children again, especially now that they had new friends and roots in the community. Charles said he did not want to be without us for nine months. There was no middle ground.

Sifting through the clutter of the past, I would remember, discard, reorder, and often wonder how such randomness fits into a Christian framework. I was beginning to understand why I'd stayed away from church at a time when I was crying out for a spiritual underpinning. I wasn't yet ready to believe that God was listening to my prayers. Quite the opposite—I felt my faith being tested like Job's.

But the clouds were slowly lifting, and I could believe that pain, guilt, and suffering, like hope, were all part of the eternal plan. I just needed to keep reminding myself that God works in ways too mysterious to fathom. And the fact that because I couldn't seem to break through to Him simply means I was unable to envision a transcendent order of reality. Maybe patience was what I needed to get better at.

The magnolia trees along Lincoln Road were filled with birdsong and velvety white blossoms. That was cause for rejoicing. I heard the Boston Symphony play Beethoven's "C Major

Mass," then voices from the Tanglewood Festival Chorus filled the hall with a triumphant message. I knew that someday I would become a believer again. The words *Deum de Deo, Lumen de Lumine* faded into gentle harmonies…

*Sanctus, Sanctus, Sanctus,*
*Dominus Deus Sabaoth…*
*Hosanna in excelsis.*

*Goose at Sandy Pond*

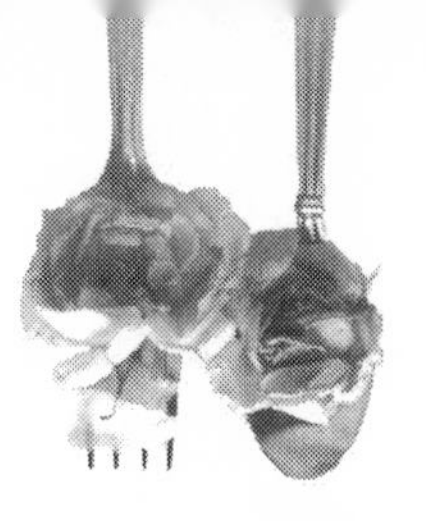

# chapter twelve

The kaleidoscope continued to spin, and, in every frame, I saw family and friends who were big on loyalty, fair play, and concern for others but too often skirted their own feelings.

One day, I said to Cecily, "You know, your sickness has taught us better ways of looking at things. Now I'm thinking of my needs and everyone else's feelings, too."

She smiled. Just then, Veronica, a health aide, popped her head in to tell Cecily she was wanted at the nursing station for her "meds."

Moments later, she was back, and I asked her, "What do you wish for now?"

In a voice so low that I had to strain to hear, she said, "Good health."

I didn't think she would ask for happiness ever after. I thought it would be for permission to leave the hospital. I hugged her closely, thinking of my fragile child asking for something that had been so abundantly hers in childhood.

More and more often, she spoke about her fears of becoming dependent on McLean. It was a safe place where she got a great deal of attention. Few mental illnesses are as attention dependent as anorexia nervosa.

In the late seventies, psychiatrists were encrusted with accreditation and specialty status and articles after their names in medical journals. They used technical terms and thin threads to follow elusive concepts back into the misty past. Too many neglected to cultivate a measure of empathy for the parents *as allies in the battle for their child's health.*

I asked for a meeting to discuss the matter of Cecily's therapist. Dr. C brought along two colleagues. One was a health aide who looked so young I wondered how anyone so unblemished by life could point us in the direction of resolution or insight. The third member of the hospital team was a psychiatric "cluster chief" (a position I never did figure out) who was about my age and one of very few women high on the McLean staff. She seemed strangely untoughened by her daily contact with human misery and smiled warmly on being introduced.

I felt a little courage returning. I told them Cecily was regressing since last summer, that she was still unable to express her needs, that she remained isolated. Worst of all, she refused to discuss her feelings with her therapist. Dr. C presented the hospital side, a solid block rallying to the support of McLean's own.

"Cecily's case is a complex one," the doctor began. "Consistency is the really important ingredient. Even when she won't speak to Dr. S, therapy is happening on one level."

They all seemed to find cheer in the fact that her therapist refused to be pushed aside. Cluster chief said something to the effect that liking your therapist isn't all that important. Trust is what matters.

"But she doesn't trust him either," I said. "She tells me she never lets him know any of her real feelings. Why not a woman therapist?"

There was silence and regrouping. I knew females were a rarity on the staff. Then one of the group returned to the matter of consistency. "The moment anyone gets to what really bothers Cecily, she turns away. She does it with everyone. What's really needed here is follow-through."

He was right about Cecily turning away from anyone getting too close. That is part of the anorexic syndrome. Most anorexics are terrified at the thought of having an intimate relationship, while at the same time unconsciously longing for one. Ambivalence follows them like a shadow. It takes a skillful therapist to gain the confidence of these reclusive patients.

To respond intuitively to their needs requires not only professional skills, but also, I believe, empathy and sensitivity. Perhaps it was too much to expect these qualities in one person, but I did feel that three years was an excessively long trial period. It was increasingly difficult to remain a mute witness to Cecily's silent rages and self-destructive episodes while her hospital kept cashing our huge checks.

Any way I looked at it, I could never understand how therapy could be helpful when the power base was so unequal, the boundaries so rigid. I remember one meeting Charles and I had with Dr. S. What came through to both of us was his aloof manner. When he spoke of separation and independence as the goal for Cecily, it felt to me like mother bashing. Wouldn't a woman therapist be better able to repair the disconnections through mutual empathy and an understanding of the reality of being female?

It is not unusual for an anorexic to mistrust her therapist. She is angry with him, on the one hand, for not understanding her anguish, and, on the other hand, she denies that there are any problems and tries to manipulate him.

It is generally believed that the two necessary requisites in a therapist are experience and knowledge of the disorder, but I have reservations about the former. Each therapist must start somewhere, but to admit to inexperience means: to be open to the possibility of failure, to be willing to discard a treatment modality that's not working, and to be a good listener, one who is open to all subtleties in the patient, even in the silences.

Not infrequently, a therapist feels helpless and angry in the face of the anorexic's manipulations and the parents' distress. They're apt to move too fast, often in the area of sexuality, further wounding the anorexic's emerging sense of self. In order to know when to move into these sensitive areas does not require experience as much as intuition, empathy, and a flexible style.

Cecily was a noncompliant patient. I went to see her that week, but she refused my visit. She said she wouldn't speak to me until we promised to take her out of the hospital. A nurse, trying to cheer me up, said she'd gained two pounds. I knew it was not a matter of weight. Since her arrival in the intensive care unit, there had been little real change in her underlying issues. If left to her own devices, she would surely continue to plummet downward.

By the summer of 1977, Cecily was still without a therapist and was hoping for a woman. Jay, a thirty-one-year-old bearded Vietnam vet, had stepped into a pseudo-therapist role. He was a mental health aide with empathy and a sense of humor. In the literature, I could find no mention whatsoever of humor, but I came to see this as an important quality, especially when dealing with the anorexic patient, who is deficient in reality testing and takes everything as deadly serious. A gentle teasing and joking around was part of Jay's arsenal, along with skirmishes into poetry and fables.

Cecily liked his laid-back style.

"She's not having those wild fluctuations anymore," Jay told me. "But she's really down. This may be the time when she comes up to face her fears and follow them back to their source."

In a letter dated November 5, 1977, I wrote:

*Dearest Cecily,*

*You might think this sounds strange, but I've come to believe that even despair can be a stage in one's growth. Maybe if you look at it that way, what you're going through now won't seem quite so bleak and helpless.*

*You can lick this terror—I know you can with the same stubborn determination you used in almost starving yourself to death. Today I am remembering China's Chairman Mao, who said, "A journey of a thousand miles begins with a single step."*

*I will be watching from a distance for this route to self-discovery must be traveled alone. Frightening as this sounds, it is the price of being grown-up and worth it, I believe. Hope someday you will, too.*

*God go with you always.*

*With love,*

*Mum*

Cecily never mentioned the letter, but soon on her wall I saw a Chairman Mao poster about his thousand-mile journey. Chris had found the poster at the Harvard Coop. Across the bottom, he scrawled, *Cecily, be sure to wear sturdy shoes.* He was the child who kept a sense of humor throughout Cecily's illness.

Later that same month, Cecily sent me a poem:

*You were always there to talk to when everything was bright*
*You were there to cry to when nothing seemed right*
*You were there to catch me*
*When my world was tumbling down*
*And that is why for YOU I'll always be around.*

I saw the poem as a promise that she wouldn't self-destruct, that she wasn't aiming for suicide. Anorexics eat to fill an emotional vacuum, and then, unable to stop, become racked by self-loathing, realizing that once again they have lost control over their lives. To be in a hospital, watched over and medicated, must breed that same sense of helplessness.

One time, after Cecily singed her arm badly with a cigarette, I asked her about the voices in her head.

"They're always warring around inside my head," she said. "I hate war."

"Me too," I told her.

The voices could be terrifying, often conflicting, some yelling at her to eat more, others to not eat anything.

A few days later, Jay very patiently explained "primary process" to me: "It's the irrational in Cecily's head," he said. "Voices, fantasies, dreams, all telling her in different forms how to battle against the secondary process."

"And that is?"

"The message the staff and her family are giving her, but somehow she stops believing it. Then the pressure builds and keeps on building, until it vents in an act like cutting or burning."

Her siblings at home believed she could perfectly well control her impulses. Frustrated and angry, they stayed away from the hospital after one of her self-harming acts. Rob stopped writing to her. Her life grew narrower and narrower.

Cecily's journey was helping me understand the values I inherited—tamping down one's feelings, keeping the peace, and avoiding confrontations. But it was like changing the rules in the middle of the game. Where did that leave a fifty-six-year-old woman without a rulebook?

For three years, change was the only constant. Programs, therapists, medications were begun and discarded. On her worst of days, I thought this was all there was to life. As Heraclitus knew long ago, "Nothing endures but change."

As Cecily's weight inched up slowly towards the mid-nineties, panic and a sense of foreboding followed. Her room at McLean was stripped, the record player and records removed because the staff didn't trust her around sharp edges.

I met with Greg, who was still our social worker, and we talked about the self-destructive episodes, the vomiting and the element of free will. He thought it was significant that she could control the purging when on "specials" (when an aide was an arm's length away around the clock).

We hoped the compulsive attitudes would fade as soon as she learned acceptable ways of showing anger. She longed for control over her life, but despaired of the possibility as long as she was institutionalized. And she had to be institutionalized as long as she was hurting herself.

Each time she asked permission to move home, it was turned down. She was a self-destructive, high-risk patient. The implication: home was where it all began.

❧

Two years after Cecily's admission to McLean, Charles suggested we go to Paris for six weeks. He needed to continue his academic research at the Bibliothèque Nationale and thought we might be able to patch up our lives far removed from the crisis atmosphere of a psychiatric hospital.

It had all rolled down to a choice between degrees of hurt, between a child and a husband, risking a life or a marriage. The sensual side of me wished to stay in my marriage and travel. The maternal side demanded that I remain close to my daughter. I thought that my disappearance for any length of time would be seen by her as a final rejection. That the barely-flickering life spark in her exhausted body would extinguish if there was no mother waiting for her when she came home.

Loss: the memory of the way I felt after my first husband's death. Fear: the prospect of taking responsibility for myself and shuffling into old age, alone and unloved. These images broke over me, leaving me spent, but slowly a new way of making decisions came to me.

I was seeing random pieces of the whole clearly for the first time in years. I couldn't be responsible for the pain and anger of a husband who saw my work in the eating disorder field as a barrier keeping us apart. To him, my work was an obsession and a real threat to the marriage. To me, it was a way of keeping afloat, a lifeline.

I knew I could stand up to Charles's anger while holding fast to a selfhood in the process of becoming. In the stark gray light of that long New England winter, I saw that the best I could do for my husband and my family was to jettison the old feelings of dependency and start to think of myself.

Not an easy task, I realized. With my multiple selves over the years, I turned to my journals in search of the essential me.

> *I told him I'm going to Selma, and he is infuriated, can't understand my leaving all my responsibilities as wife and mother, take off at some risk for a cause that certainly wasn't mine. Odd, I think, the cause is mine, I think I've known it all along, the need to witness, maybe even in some infinitesimal way lessen the pain of others. Maybe that's why I found myself in Europe during the war. Seems to me that Jews, blacks, whites—whomever—share a common humanity, a vision of a fairer world. Then why can't I make him understand?*

Starting up my Volvo, I was captured by a recording of "We Shall Overcome," and suddenly I was back on a broad street in Selma, Alabama. About forty of us had been arrested for taking part in the march for black voter registration in the white section of town. We were waiting for Sheriff Jim Clark with his dogs and the bus that would take us to jail. I saw a white woman standing in the doorway across the street pointing a rifle at us and yelling words I couldn't make out. I was caught in an emotional whirlpool that I couldn't close off. *Will I ever overcome someday?*

If even one of Cecily's therapists or doctors had hinted at a sense of indecision, we might have explored alternatives for her. But the professional consensus was always unanimous, and my self-esteem was so low, I was unable to make a clear-headed decision about Cecily's care on my own. I was the controlling mother, and Charles, the distant father. Together, we were a formidable impediment on the path to autonomy and separation, which were McLean's goals for Cecily.

One day, a mental health worker talked to me about Cecily's disruptive behavior. "The staff hate using restraints on your daughter. It's for her protection."

"It's really gooning," Cecily said. "It's easy for them to give me medication by needle when I'm all tied up."

Were her symptomatic excesses a normal response to an intolerable situation? Day after day, year after year, from early morning until late at night, her actions were controlled by others, her privacy invaded in countless humiliating and often painful ways. If that was reality, small wonder she tried to fight it.

It is generally accepted that psychiatric intervention can't be effective for the anorexic patient until minimal weight is achieved. The chance of intervention ever being meaningful is greatly reduced if this early period of hospitalization is mishandled. Several months were wasted at the start of Cecily's treatment trying to get her to cooperate. She was assigned a health aide but no psychiatrist. It was during this stage that the disastrous path of Cecily's hospitalization might have been changed for the better. Had a woman doctor with the female's natural compassion taken over her case, Cecily's story might have been very different. Sadly, I did not find out until much later that there was such a person on the McLean staff.

Somebody should have explained to Cecily in her first week at McLean that no one was going to let her die and that no one was going to let her get fat, but she had to take nourishment—that was nonnegotiable. The method was up to her. Giving her options might have encouraged her to be an active participant in the success of her program. Even measures that seemed coercive, such as nasogastric tube feedings and locked bathrooms, if explained beforehand and presented as part of a contract, can be seen as "safe" rituals.

Cecily was not appointed a therapist until *after* the emotional scarring of intubation occurred. It came as a shock to me when I realized that McLean, a pioneering force in the field of mental health, routinely prescribed restraints in the form of sensory deprivation, restrictive camisoles, lengthy isolation periods in a quiet room, and hydrotherapy.

It was years later, through a book about McLean Hospital, that I was able to picture the use of wet packs, a treatment used to pacify agitated patients. It entailed wrapping them in cold (48–56°F) wet sheets. The effect was divided into action (the cooling of the skin) and thermal reaction (skin becomes warmer and muscles relax). But hypothermia was a risk.[10]

So was death of the spirit. It occurred to me after reading Alex Beam's dispassionate view of wet packs that he had never actually witnessed a patient undergoing the treatment nor spoken to anyone later about the experience. Had he met with Cecily, he might have chosen a different title for his book—instead of *Gracefully Insane*, something more like *Barbarism in the Mental Hospital.*

I wondered why no one tried holding and calming Cecily. This was a private institution. We were paying "specials," an exorbitant rate, to have them watch over our daughter. It was scarcely surprising that her anger ran rampant in the hospital or that later attempts to turn her program around failed. The control measures were excessively harsh, the understanding was too little, the pain too great.

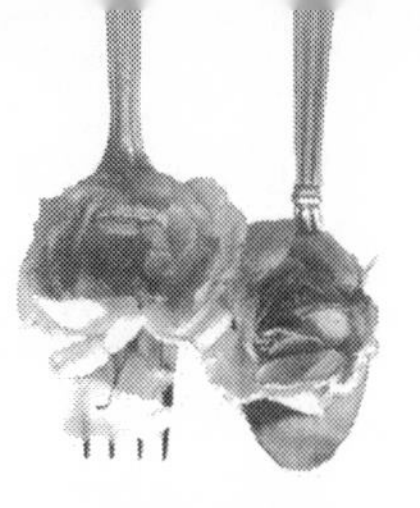

# chapter thirteen

Behind McLean is a large, open area that was enclosed by a high, un-scalable brick wall. In the winter, it was bleak and mostly shaded, but in the summer warblers and finches flitted through the leafy branches of the tall trees. There was a torn volleyball net and a rusted swing set in one corner. Private hospitals like McLean made little use of their natural setting. They rarely recommended fresh air and exercise for their patients—so different from the approach used in Swiss sanitariums, where exercise was an important part of treatment programs.

When Dr. Hilde Bruch consulted with the McLean staff on Cecily's case in January 1976, she recommended that her treatment stay the same with one caveat: Cecily should be allowed walks on the hospital grounds as often as possible. But this was never carried out and so another opportunity was missed. By concentrating on the pathology to the exclusion of all else, there was little chance Cecily would stumble on any fleeting pleasure.

Traces of the grounds' former elegance—it was designed by Frederick Law Olmsted—were still visible, but through Cecily's tightly meshed window screen, she could only make out a small sliver of sky and cars in the parking lot. She was too sick for insight therapy, we were told. That, I could understand, but why were no creative ways to lighten her mood explored—walks on the grounds, yoga, journal writing, or music therapy?

Hospital staff often told us that Cecily would die unless she remained in a secure facility. The implicit message: home wasn't an option because that is where the illness originated. I was angry at the doctors and the review boards that looked at Cecily and her treatment plan. Each time, they decided it would be best for her to stay at McLean.

For the first year, I understood this "best interest" clause, but as time went on, I thought the chance of the success of her treatment program should be weighed against the negative effects of long-term institutionalization. We were encouraged to keep her on at McLean as long as we could continue to pay the bills. If we hadn't had the money, I'm sure the hospital recommendation would have been quite different.

So anger crept slowly around the edges of my life, and with it a slow-building exhaustion. Looking at the natural forces of change during my lifetime—the Great Depression, World War II, the chaotic sixties—it was evident that in any storm some are affected profoundly while others float along unscathed.

My three middle children, Chris, Nick, and Cecily, were teenagers in the sixties, and all experienced rough passages through adolescence. Rob, Roz, and Josh, on the other hand, faced their teenage years at a relatively peaceful period in our nation's history, and scarcely felt its touch.

Still, over time, it became clear to me that the rage I felt over the failure of others led back to me, for I, the mother, was the first person Cecily turned to in her life. Now, in my mid-fifties, I had to face my own failure as a mother. I was upset at myself for not making an early call to the Menninger Clinic in Topeka when I first saw signs of Cecily's *isolating* behaviors, an early marker of psychological distress.

I fumed at the doctors involved in Cecily's case, who never told me about relational-cultural therapy (RCT). A feminist approach based on the work of Dr. Jean Baker Miller, RCT was being explored by a few courageous women at McLean in the late seventies. The Stone Center Group at Wellesley College had at its base two concepts: individuals grow through and toward connection, not separation; and mutual empathy is at the core of all growth. As this stood in marked contrast to the Freudian model, I understand why this was kept from me.

I did meet with one key associate, Dr. Janet Surrey, shortly before she left McLean. I learned that she had been interviewed for the position of Cecily's therapist in 1974 and was rejected because she was new on the staff and considered too inexperienced for such a challenging case. Another opportunity lost.

I imagined her working with Cecily on a two-track system. On one hand, disorder of the self, on the other, relief of the eating disorder symptoms. The latter was an area never addressed by anyone on the McLean staff. How could I not feel betrayed by these Freudian-based male clinicians with their own biases, backgrounds, and value systems, who held such power over our lives for so long?

And so I raged on behalf of myself and all mothers of eating-disordered children who were viewed by clinicians steeped in Freudian theory as the primal cause of their daughters' sickness. I saw Cecily's treatment as a sign of McLean's blindness at the highest clinical level.

*The McLean staff had reached its goal, and Cecily, after over four years of psychic investment in self-starvation, has lost. Everyone—staff, patients, family—tell her she looks super terrific. How come then she feels so badly? She senses trickery, feels herself drifting rapidly out of control. If she can reach 90, what is to stop her from ballooning up to 190? It's a no-win situation, she realizes, this choice between anorexia and obesity. For to plummet down off their arbitrarily selected weight plateau means to stay on in the hospital, force-fed like a goose, and day after mind-numbing day, growing more angry, more helpless, more fat. It means they'll expect her to keep on changing, and they won't see her as special anymore, undeserving of attention. And, no matter how they explain it to her, she knows all the nameless terrors will not fade into the woodwork simply because she has hit 90 pounds. Such a change means only one thing to her—that her true needs and insecurities will be visible, exposed like her new rolls of flesh for all to see. Best, she thinks, to stick with the specters that have haunted her sleeping and waking hours for so long than to feed her emotional hungers and confront her feelings. With companions like rage, guilt, and self-hate, who needs real friends? Or food, either, for that matter.*

—Notes from my talks with Cecily, 1978

The new program for Cecily, in September 1978, was a combination of behavior modification and assertiveness training, and it wasn't working. She was still having difficulty forming meaningful relationships, though some of her anorexic symptoms were fading. She was better able to express her feelings and was maintaining her weight in the low nineties. Anything to avoid the tube.

Her teeth, yellow and hurting, had eroded down to the gum line. I made an appointment with a dentist who said that her teeth were losing enamel because of the acid in stomach bile and they needed to be capped or maybe even pulled. The surgery was performed. Rob and Nick, home from L.A., accompanied her. They stopped on the way back to McLean to fill her pain medication prescription. She took several codeine pills in the car, and, at the hospital they gave her more, which precipitated a bad reaction—tremors, slurred speech, and difficulty in walking or standing. So for the fourth year, she was not allowed home for Christmas.

Charles flew to Dallas for a meeting of French historians. Afterward I joined him in Rockport, a small fishing village on the Texas coast that was famed for its varied bird life. We took a boat down the Intracoastal Waterway to the wintering ground of the whooping crane. It was unforgettably beautiful—adults and young feeding in the shallows across a barrier reef, a cloud of white with scarlet crowns and black wingtips. An exaltation of hope.

In our absence, Cecily cut her arm again. She told us she didn't believe she would ever be free of the hospital. Charles told her it was this sort of behavior that kept her stuck, an old record that she tuned out. It was so disheartening. The cuts didn't respond well to antibiotics, and her down mood continued.

Aware of her shrinking options, I sent off a letter to an orthomolecular facility in Long Island for inpatients asking if they would take her. When her acceptance arrived, she was excited. The McLean staff, with Freudian single-track vision, was not optimistic, but the director of the hospital, a burly big-spirited Texan said to me, "Go ahead and try it, Mrs. Warner. We're for anything that works."

I found Cecily in a long, white cotton dress and told her how nice she looked.

"White's my favorite color," she said.

White—ascetic and uncompromising—symbolized the perfectionist state anorexics continually strive for.

"I don't need people in my life," she told me. "I'm going to be a nun."

So many mood swings. One day, totally alert, she delighted in inventing palindromes with her father. Then, the very next day, I would find her sitting on her bed, barefoot, light years away, clutching a gray McLean blanket around her like a carapace.

One day, her hair was brushed and shining and her voice had lost the thick, toneless quality I associated with her medication. She told me they had cut down on her Loxapine and she was getting privileges to visit in the rooms of other patients. She was more hopeful, but the idea of a new hospital was scary.

As we talked about it, the sound of raised voices tumbled towards us from the community room at the end of the hallway. Often I had trouble separating the sound of soap operas on the TV from many of the personal dramas at McLean. Both flowed nonstop at the same high emotional pitch. Maybe tuning out made sense after all.

There was a knock at the door. The staff was having one of their periodic housekeeping exercises. An aide asked me to take home a carton of stuff Cecily wasn't using. Someone had already gathered up an assortment of clothing, records, books, several on diet and nutrition, yet there was also *The Satanic Bible*, works of Jorge Luis Borges, and Zelda Fitzgerald's *Save Me the Waltz*.

Cecily's euphoria over the chance at a new hospital was short-lived. She had a psychotic reaction that developed quickly. When I went to see her, she couldn't speak, but then slowly, tonelessly asked me questions about our family. She couldn't remember the names of her brothers or sisters. The light from the hallway tinted her skin the color of faded wisteria. Her eyes glistened dully like pale washed-out pools. We couldn't connect at all. The nurse told me she was suffering from a form of transient amnesia, which is a psychic escape from overwhelming anxiety. In her case, the anxiety seemed to be rooted in the thought of leaving behind some of her favorite staff members.

The Long Island hospital, hearing of this regressive condition and fearing she might refuse their megavitamin therapy, reconsidered and decided against her admission. Cecily was so low she hardly reacted. The McLean staff recommended that she be transferred to another secure facility. No one believed she could live more than a short while without the strictest supervision. The Metropolitan State Hospital up the road was selected. Jay would continue as her therapist.

After four and a half years, and a king's ransom, McLean had signaled failure.

The staff of the state hospital wasn't able to handle the needs of their new patient. We were all despondent as Cecily's weight started plummeting. It was then that Dr. Gordon Winchell, our family's physician, intervened and wrote out orders for her to be transferred to a medical unit of Concord's Emerson Hospital.

Would this be our first sliver of hope?

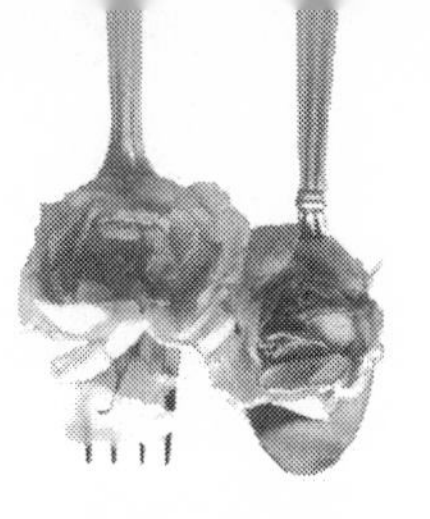

# chapter fourteen

Cecily was at Emerson Hospital for a brief stay. Then she was discharged and came home after being in a mental hospital for four years.

She enrolled in a nurse's aide program at the Minuteman Technical School. Upon completion of the course, she was assigned to a Jesuit hospital in Weston. She went to work late at night in an oversized white uniform. She was not sure she had the strength to make it through the eight-hour shift. Her supervisor felt she needed more time to recover strength. It was another rejection that triggered a new spate of binging behavior.

Cecily returned to Emerson Hospital six times—for wrist cutting, alcohol overdose, malnutrition (at one point dropping to 59 pounds, her lowest weight since childhood), and a life-threatening electrolyte imbalance. The hospitalizations were brief. Sometimes she was on the psychiatric unit; other times the pediatric, where the atmosphere was cheerful and calm. Several of the pediatric nurses were touched by this waif-like patient. They took the place of health aides she had grown to trust at McLean. Other aides were less able to cope with coaxing the stubborn patient into following a program that would save her life. Dr. Winchell explained Cecily's case to the staff, but it was hard to justify taking up a sought-after bed. Anorexic patients aren't cost-effective for the suburban hospital, which had no comprehensive treatment plan for them.

In spite of many difficulties, the healing inched ahead.

One day, Cecily wrote me a letter and left it on my desk:

> *Dear Mum,*
>
> *No matter how I look at it, from whatever angle, it appears to be a strange and brutally invasive experience for a kid—which is what I was. It seems so close. The nightmarish quality. I want to believe that the professionals in charge of my treatment, whoever they were, knew what they were doing. I don't want to doubt them, but it still seems to me, they kept my body alive at the cost of the spirit. Maybe I was never meant to leave the hospital, so it didn't matter. Everything and I mean EVERYTHING was done AGAINST my will. Forcefully. I had no say whatsoever in anything that was going on around me and if I didn't cooperate I was punished. I can't talk about it for it is hard to find a way to describe such an experience. It hurt so much, the pain is still so real, and I feel I gained absolutely nothing from those endless years. It only taught me that when people say, "We care," it really means, "We have to hurt you." My head may forget the messages I received day in and day out, but I doubt my heart will forget the hurtful reality of a hospitalization in which the treatment left more scars than the disease. I guess some things you just never understand.*
>
> *Still, at this stage, I know I'll never give up as long as I have the freedom I spent so many years dreaming about. It may be a very long time before I'll be able to trust anyone, but*

*I really believe if I keep working on it, someday I'll be able to look people in the eye, trust again, and feel human.*

*Love,*

*Cecily*

This outcry was an important first step. She was slowly getting ready to talk more about her treatment.

When Cecily was strong enough to leave Emerson Hospital, Dr. Winchell came up with what seemed like a dismal plan: a stay in the home for the elderly. The benefits soon became apparent: small portions and bland meals always served on time gave structure to her days. Her evenings were filled with the presence of an understanding roommate, Irene Sigler, a twenty-one-year-old cystic fibrosis patient who had known abuse, deprivation, and pain. In spite of or maybe because of this, life was valuable to her and each new morning a new gift. In this environment, Cecily wasn't the focus of attention, and she started reaching out to others more needy than herself.

Charles and I talked constantly about how to give Cecily more freedom while setting clear limits. She would spend all her allowance on large quantities of food and sometimes bottles of wine, which she squirreled away in her bedroom behind a locked door. We tried to stay calm when a quart of orange juice was consumed in the middle of the night, along with everything we might have wanted for breakfast.

Once again, we were walking on eggshells.

Our fears were real and so were our frustrations. By organizing the normal activities of the household around her self-destructive behaviors, we were acknowledging weakness in the face of her greater power. By adjusting our needs to her erratic moods, we were giving out confusing signals like before.

The other children stayed away.

On good days, I waited patiently for her cues, the countless nonverbal ways in which she would permit me to enter her personal space. Other days, almost any casual remark would result in a hasty withdrawal behind a slammed bedroom door. But gradually I grew to understand the ancient disharmonies and hurts.

Cecily's bathroom overflowed with moisturizing creams—dry skin, oily skin, scented, unscented, organic, lanolin-based—and conditioners, bath oils, toiletries of all kinds.

Finally deciding it was confrontation time, I suggested she cut back on her purchases until she finished the surplus she already had.

"All right, I won't buy anything ever again."

There it was again, that all-or-nothing attitude. Keeping calm, I talked about how to budget for essentials, but there was an anger between us, cold and implacable.

"Last week, you were checking on my pills, Mum. Now you're saying I can't buy stuff at the drugstore."

"And next week," I cut in, "you'll be upset when your allowance is gone three days after you get it. I really wish that—"

"I had another mother…anyone but you."

In the past, I would have turned away in hurt and left the room. "Well, you don't," I said. "I'm the only mother you've got, so you'd better learn how to deal with me."

I was mad at my daughter and mad at myself for having to babysit a grown-up. Was I at a turning point?

*My center is giving away, my right is pulled back, situation excellent, I'm attacking.*

This sentence was in a dispatch sent by Marshal Ferdinand

Foch to French headquarters during the battle of the Marne during the First World War. I found the quote scribbled on a piece of paper on Charles's desk. It felt like a message from God about going on the offensive.

Soon after, our neighbors Dana and Barbara Atchley came by and told us about their daughter, Abigail, who had died of an overdose the previous year. Her diagnosis, extremely rare at the time, was bulimia. She had left a note for her parents at a motel north of Boston, part of which read, *Living is just too hard.* We talked that night about how slow we were to see the turmoil in our own daughters and how little information on eating disorders was available in the media, in schools, even among healthcare professionals.

Dana said, "My brother just founded an eating disorder support organization in New Jersey. Can you see yourself doing something like that here in New England?"

Couldn't Dana see I was running on empty? Then the words of Marshal Foch came back to me—*situation excellent, I am attacking.* I heard myself saying, "Yes, yes, I can."

"Great, I'll handle incorporation, taxes, balancing the books, and the business end. You do the rest."

Over the years, anorexia nervosa had spread across the lines of age, gender, and social standing.[11] About forty people came to our first meeting of the Anorexia Nervosa Aid Society (ANAS), which we soon renamed Anorexia Bulimia Care (ABC). That evening, the mother of an anorexic spoke of going through the dark night of the soul, feeling lost and alone. Parents around her nodded, recognizing her journey as their own.

The outline of a plan for how the organization would be structured was forming in my mind—anorexics and bulimics meeting with a "recovering" leader, sharing their fears and compulsions, and learning how to get their needs met without starving or stuffing.

I thought I could handle the job of executive director if I had an active support team to back me up. What struck me later is that those first board members took such a risk on me. I didn't have even one psychology course in my academic background and no clue how to run a nonprofit or self-help agency. To this day, I find their trust in me amazing and humbling.

I will always be grateful to Dr. Eugene Piazza, an early researcher in the field of eating disorders at Boston Children's Hospital. He was the first doctor courageous enough to join our Professional Advisory Board. Also from Children's Hospital like Dr. Piazza, Dr. Alexander Eliot helped immeasurably in many areas and chaired our annual conferences. Dr. David Herzog, at a period when he was busy formulating plans for the Harvard Eating Disorder Center at Massachusetts General Hospital, joined early on and remained an active and insightful presence, as did Catherine Steiner-Adair, later my graduate mentor.

Many others followed, each making valuable contributions. They were all interested in early intervention and seeing eating disorder cases reduced and the quality of life for the symptomatic improved. After that first meeting in Lincoln's First Parish Church, it hit me that the word *cure* was in no one's lexicon yet. At rare times in one's life, there is a real break in a pattern, a change that makes one look at events and behaviors from a different angle. The turning point for me was heading up our new eating disorder support organization.

After I began my advocacy work, Charles's depression, which appeared first as a reaction to Cecily's problems, took on a different target.

I can never forget his question to me one day: "Do you have to be Auschwitz-thin in this family to get your attention? That damn hotline is always ringing for you, Pat."

*Charles is really uptight. I try to organize the domestic machinery, but I won't do the one thing he wants: give up on ABC. Cecily also resents my extra-familial preoccupations, but in some way I can't explain, seems to be growing more real. Last night, sitting on the edge of the bed, brushing her hair, she moved easily from a discussion of split ends to Rob's father—"what was he like," she asks? How did I handle the pain and emptiness after his death? Did I ever want to die? I think that seeing me as open and vulnerable frees her to be more honest with her feelings, for we talked a long time about separation and loss, about all the moves in her childhood, about the death of her grandmother and two close friends, Irene from cystic fibrosis, and Steve, a McLean patient who committed suicide.*

*I talked as much as she did and at the end, told her I was beginning to find myself an interesting topic of conversation—and that we should have this kind of sharing more often.*

—My Journal, May 5, 1979

To Cecily, my work at Anorexia Bulimia Care meant I was no longer available to take her shopping, to the movies, wherever. My absorption in helping others put doubts in her mind about my love for her.

"You spend more time talking to patients than you do me," she hissed after overhearing a phone conversation with a new ABC member. "My mother has stolen my disease," she told her brother.

*Dear Mum,*

*You are right. We really should talk more about you. Most of the time, you are quiet and talk so little about yourself (you're getting better, though), and that's because you're always thinking about everyone else. Well, I just want you to know I'm thinking about you because I love you and worry about you. Sound familiar? Like mother...like daughter.*

*I would like to see you when you're tired and being unfairly treated, lash back, get bitchy, and stand up for yourself. I'm giving free analysis because tomorrow you'll be 58. And it dawned on me that you must have been 36 when I was born, which means it's not too late for me to raise a child who I will love and who will love me too.*

*And I want you to know that I'm so very sorry if I hurt you. I've been hurt so much, not by you, though, but when I yell at you I'm really yelling at those others who did the hurting. You are gentle and kind, and I know you can absorb my anger and not walk away. I, of course, know that this isn't right, so I'm working on changing this scene, now I finally recognize it.*

*I respect you, Mum. You're one hell of a soldier—and a mother too. Happy Birthday, and many, many, many more.*

*With much love,*

*Cecily*

This letter helped me see myself through my daughter's eyes. She gave me advice, which was not much different from what I was hearing from other quarters. I must be more assertive, decide what is rightfully mine—blame, anger, resentment—and deal with it openly. Over the years, I'd been defined by someone else. That passivity fit me like a glove. The pattern had been set early on. I never revealed what I was feeling inside. It was a learned response familiar to many of my generation. It took my daughter's disease for me to understand the parts of my legacy I needed to change.

I had been too close, too involved with my daughter, while Charles moved further away on his own path. Cecily was acutely sensitive, picking up on her father's distancing and aligning herself with me in the uneasy love-hate relationship of the Oedipal child.

She was still in a battle for control of her life. While her peers and siblings moved towards separation and independence, she was stuck at home.

*Dear Mum,*

*Tonight can you help me plan a meal—something sustaining? Then, I won't be feeling so bored and lonely. Thinking about you is making me feel better already.*

*Cecily*

This note, left on the kitchen table, was a slight move forward, because, like all anorexics, Cecily was unable to separate her nutritional needs from her emotional ones. Asking for help in food planning was a step in the right direction.

As for the seizures, Dr. Winchell wrote on September 2, 1982:

*This is the fifth EEG local and awake on a 25-year-old female. The patient is not on medication. Photic driving at 10, 15, and 16 flashes. Impression: Normal EEG.*

*Normal*—what a glorious word.

But any reason to cheer was short-lived. Ten days later, her binging and purging returned and she was back at Emerson Hospital with a low potassium count.

Cecily telephoned early one morning from the hospital to say that she had a day pass and that, instead of having four hours at home, she would like to go to Cambridge and eat at the Blue Parrot.

On the way into town, she chatted nervously about all the things she wanted to do that day. She had a list. "I've written it all down so I won't forget," she said.

I worried that she might be overwhelmed by the sudden freedom.

The Blue Parrot catered to Harvard students with a taste for foreign dishes. Waiting for our order, she glanced at the people at nearby tables. "Do you think they know…I'm a mental patient?" she asked.

"How could they? But they might think you're on a diet."

"There you go," she said, "lecturing about my weight."

Increasingly, I felt confrontation was necessary, even therapeutic. It was the change in Cecily's personality that kept catching me off guard. A happy, effervescent girl, quick to laugh and slow to anger, was now filled with mood shifts. I knew this darkness was not my daughter but her illness.

"Sorry, Mum. It's not only with you and Dad. At the hospital, they call me a 'spoiled brat.'"

"Who says that?"

"The patients. They think I have no right to be sick with the money we have."

We returned home to find Charles in the driveway folding up his telescope. He could talk endlessly about umbrae and penumbrae and of the sun's instability, but he became speechless when puzzling over his daughter's moods and feelings.

Ordinarily, I would have peered through the telescope too, but I was tired and depressed. I walked into the kitchen and stood waiting for the water in the teakettle to boil. I began to make vichyssoise for dinner, placing chives, leeks, potatoes and a jar of condensed chicken stock on the kitchen counter.

Why didn't Charles join us in those rare times Cecily had permission to leave the hospital grounds?

A one-year position at the University of Iowa opened up for Charles. He was asked to fill in again for his friend Alan Steere in the European History slot.

That year when he was away, he wrote and phoned sporadically. His students were challenging. He was back researching his Napoleon book. He had met his favorite astronomer, Professor James Van Allen, and was learning a lot about rotation belts and galaxies.

One call I remember well.

"I'm beginning to see that this time apart is good for us both," he said. "It gives me a fresh perspective on Cecily. It makes me realize how grateful I am to you. All that you do on the home front. Thanks, Old Wagon.'"

"Old Wagon" was his pet name for me.

That spring, Dr. Pope forwarded me a letter he had received from one of his colleagues:

*Dear Skip,*

*On examination, Cecily was oriented, alert, and cooperative. Neurological examination is essentially normal, though note is made of a very mild reflex asymmetry. She appears to be no longer having seizures, even though not medicated. This is something that could be consistent with post-anorexic seizure disorder—which may actually improve over time.*

*She did have an EEG two years ago, and it was said to be normal.*

*Thank you for referring Cecily. It was nice seeing her again, doing surprisingly well.*

Throughout the eighties, I spent a great deal of time speaking at school, hospitals, churches—wherever I could find an audience to talk about eating disorders. It was what I deeply wanted to do, though it might mean shuffling into old age alone and unloved.

Scenes from my marriage flickered before my eyes. I was on my way to finding my own center and saw our family against a river backdrop as Charles and I drifted along on different currents. Maybe around the bend, past the next stretch of white-water, our two currents would merge. But, for the moment, we both take turns on the river alone for different reasons.

In late August, I drove Cecily into Cambridge. All she had with her was a small backpack. She talked little on the thirty-minute trip, except to reiterate, "Mum, I'll be okay. Don't worry."

I kept reminding her, "You know you can always call."

After she disappeared into the YWCA in Central Square, a stark bleak building, I sat in the car sobbing. A policeman knocked on the window and asked if I was all right.

*Letting Cecily leave home was one of the hardest decisions I have ever had to make. Imagined horror scenes on the streets where she walks keep me awake at night. Fear hovers, too, in the daytime hours, even at those rare moments when the office is empty, the hotline silent.*

*Letters I mail to the Y are returned to me. Where is she? Who is she seeing? If only, I think, she has a support network—one not run by her mother—a friend to call, but Jay's now living in Florida. I hope she will contact Dr. Winchell and arrange for medication refills or contact Greg.*

*I continue praying: Dear God, keep her safe, bring her home. But is He listening?*

—My Journal, August 1985

In the autumn, I enrolled in a creative writing workshop at Radcliffe and at the Cambridge Adult Center, where my teacher, Mopsy Strange Kennedy, was immensely supportive. "Don't give up on your writing, Pat." So my journal kept filling up, along with a slowly building confidence that other mothers might be interested in my story.

I sent portions of my journal to an editor at Atlantic Monthly Press. He thanked me for sending it and said his top staff had given it a careful read. Their consensus: how could such a much-loved child in such a good family become so very sick?

I kept writing whenever I could, wanting so desperately to answer his question.

*When Cecily is ready for me to tell her story, I will need a different focus for my story. I won't write as the omniscient author, trying to be in the head of all the family members. I will be in my own voice—that of a mother. I know it will be very different from my first attempt. For I will be coming from a place I have never looked: the center of myself.*

—My Journal, January 1980

We moved out of our house on Sandy Pond in 1981. It was a sad day. I was moving only a short distance to a small condo near the center of town. The rain had been slicing down intermittently throughout the week, but on our last full day on Sandy Pond, the sun appeared glistening in a perfect gin-clear sky. The pink hyacinths were vibrant in the border, new leaves green on the trees—a spectrum of colors intermingling with the sadness.

It was only a short walk from my condo to our ABC office. As facilitator of the parent workshops and monthly board meetings, I increasingly sensed my inadequacies due to my lack of a psychology degree. Graduate study seemed like a wise move, but I was not sure I could handle it at sixty-two years old.

I spoke about it with Greg, Cecily's former social worker at McLean.

With the optimism of youth, he didn't equivocate. "I believe in you, Mrs. Warner."

I mailed out applications to Harvard's School of Graduate Education and to Lesley College. I was accepted at Lesley. I signed up for psychology courses, plus a family therapy course at the Cambridge Family Institute.

What became a seminal influence in shaping my thesis was a course called "Psychosocial Development in the Normal Adolescent Female" that I took at the Harvard School of Graduate Education with Dr. Carol Gilligan. In 1982, Gilligan published a seminal gender studies book, *In a Different Voice.*

I was influenced by other researchers with a feminist orientation, in particular Dr. Catherine Steiner-Adair, my thesis advisor, who helped me to see the mother's development in terms of the female's imagery of relationships. I, at least, was beginning to see the questions I needed to ask.

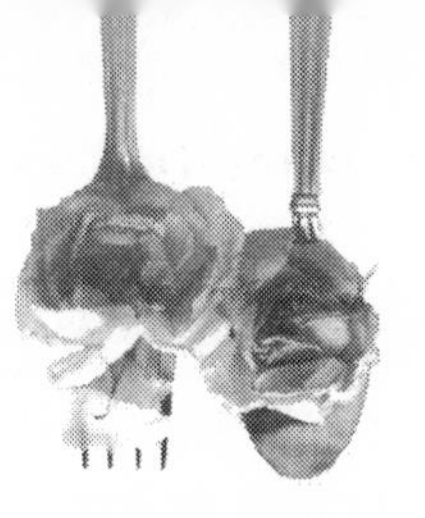

# chapter fifteen

I was poised to repeat the mistakes of the past, unless I gained a certain amount of self-knowledge. And for the longest time, I didn't. I continued along the same path as my mother, pushing down the negative feelings, playing it safe rather than exposing the areas of pain. Grief was the price I paid for attachment, for the backlog of memories, and letting go was the most difficult stage in the mourning process.

Before Cecily's hospitalization, I was always open to her demands, always fearing any kind of confrontation would push her over the edge. After she returned home, I saw that saying no is another side of caring. At first, such firmness was unsettling for us both, but, over the months running into years, I found I could live with her silence and depression, yet still provide the nurturing she needed.

Reading insatiably in the field of eating disorders, I was left curiously unsatisfied. There was always an important missing piece, which, in time, I realized was the mother's voice. In order to find it, I had to ask different questions, ones that addressed moral dilemmas, such as loss of choice and the conflict of claims between husband and wife. I already had the title for my thesis, "Eating Disorders: Mothers in Search of their Special Voice."

By giving the participants in my study a safe forum and an interviewer (me) who knew the territory and shared their pain, I hoped to find a new way to frame food abuse as a natural response to a condition of powerlessness, to the condition of being born female. I felt like the women in my study, so I included myself in the study.

I was changing now on the way to finding my own special voice. During the McLean years, I had thought that if anything went wrong with the family it was because of me, but I began to see how much Charles was like the other husbands in my study. They were all well-meaning but uninvolved in the lives of their children, which led, often, to the mothers' overinvolvement in their needy daughters.

In weaving these mothers' stories together, I saw that our struggle was between honesty and loyalty. If we tell our story, we may end up being divorced and alone, but if we do not speak out, there can be no real change in the family dynamic. My study suggested that mothers must learn to take risks, live creatively, and forge new pathways for themselves, for this is one way that we can pass on a legacy of value to our daughters, one that says less about separating and more about connection and authenticity. Otherwise, the mother senses her role is devalued, and she cannot see a way to reconcile her autonomy with her daughter's care.

My hypothesis was that if the mother can consider her own needs within the marriage or find new paths to self-worth outside the relationship, then the young daughter might also start on her way toward improved health.

One afternoon, Cecily turned up at the ABC office. She didn't want to talk about her stay at the Y. She was wearing torn blue jeans and an oversized sweatshirt, looking tired and disheveled. It was hard for me to judge her weight. Low nineties perhaps.

Upon learning that the one-room apartment above our office had been recently vacated, she asked, "Mum, can I stay there?"

I saw her asking for help as a positive sign.

Gracie Johnson, our first-floor occupant, hired Cecily as an assistant in the small antique store she ran on the ground floor.

Heading upstairs after work, Cecily sometimes stopped off at the ABC office to see if there was anything that needed doing, like collating our newsletter.

In 1985, Rob got married and brought his bride east to meet the family. We had rented a house that August on River Road in Rhinebeck, a beautiful property with gardens edging the open fields that tumbled down towards the Hudson. Rob's new bride, Suzie, was a still photographer who worked in the movies. I had planned a surprise wedding reception.

The night before the reception, Cecily and I were watching the lights flickering on the Kingston-Rhinecliff Bridge. "Mum," she said, her voice floating out of the darkness. "I'd like to go to Garrison and see Mootsie's grave."

The next day, with wildflowers we'd picked, we headed south on Route 9 in my ailing Volvo. In the graveyard of St. Philips-in-the-Highlands in Garrison-on-Hudson, Cecily, her arms filled with black-eyed Susans and Queen Anne's lace, wandered off in the direction of her grandparents' graves. I caught up with her at the Saint-Gaudens memorial, which honors my great, great-grandfather Hamilton Fish Sr., his wife and daughter. Two female figures, almost life-sized, their faces shrouded, arise out of a pink marble base, striving to transcend the present veil of sorrows.

After Cecily finished spreading flowers on our relatives' graves—Forsters, Fishes, Breeses, Keans, and Potters—we met at my parents' simple memorial stones in a secluded corner of the cemetery. Tears fell on my cheeks as I knelt on the damp, forgiving earth.

"Take care, Mother. Bobby always—Cecily, Charles, our whole family," I prayed.

We spent that night at the Bird and Bottle, a nineteenth-century coaching inn that was the scene of many Fish/Cutler happenings. For me, the most memorable event there was a dinner party hosted by my sister Judy and her husband the night before I married Charles.

Cecily asked about the guests at the party.

"Mostly relatives on my side," I told her. "A few close friends of mine and your father's, Uncle Willy, of course, Nammie and your great-grandmother, and—"

"What about Dad's father?" she interrupted. "I don't even know what to call him."

"He wasn't asked," I told her. "Your grandmother never let go of her anger. Bad enough that he showed up at Uncle Willy's and Aunt Katto's wedding."

Cecily murmured, "How sad for Dad."

The next morning we started home, visiting the family farmhouse on the old Albany Post Road. Shrubbery had grown up over the wooden tennis court and the view west overlooking the Hudson was completely blocked by trees.

"I thought the place would look, I don't know, grander," said Cecily.

Before leaving Garrison, we stopped at the Hamilton Fish

Library, which was named for my uncle and his third wife. We also stopped to look at my grandfather's house, a large Victorian brick edifice on Station Road.

"How dreary," Cecily said. "No wonder Mootsie always wanted to vacation in Newport."

Our final stop was at the Hudson River landing where, when I was child, we'd catch the boat across to West Point on Sunday afternoons to watch the army football games. My father's seats were always on the fifty-yard line. I loved the color and excitement and the marching bands more than the rough and tumble of the game.

I didn't see any signs of depressive behavior from Cecily during our trip. Still, I worried that almost any small blow to her self-esteem might propel her back into the despair that first brought her to McLean. The question, like a drumbeat, kept pounding in my head: *Will her progress stick or is she simply acting a role?*

One night, the telephone rang at home. It was Jeanie, a roommate from my boarding school days. "It's a plan, Pat. You have to say yes. A week of barging in the Canal du Midi. It's going to be fun!"

After she hung up, I pondered the word *fun*. It was such an exotic concept.

> *We moor near the walled town of Damazan. My cruise-mates decide to look for an open market in order to buy worms for Richie. I chose to stay near the site of our mooring and find myself surrounded by sheep. I approach two heavily bearded men, the berger (sheep herder) and his son. They seem truly interested in meeting an "alive" American, their first one ever. Talking in my own halting French, I make friends.*

*There is a lot of smiling. Then the herders and their sheep follow me back to the barge. Gibby painted in my journal a watercolor of the scene she titled "The Day Patricia Took Damazan."*

*Waiting for dinner on the barge's stern that evening, I watch Richie, who has made his own fishing rod, trying to connect the worms he had just been given by Bill and John, to a hook resembling an elongated paperclip. Somehow the worm container overturns and the hunt to retrieve the escapees begins—the worms looking a good deal more agile than their American cousins. The distaff group finds the scene side-splittingly hilarious.*

*Our trip is coming to an end, six days to travel 65 miles, a pace that feels absolutely right to me. Time to admire a country comfortable with its past, take note of natural loveliness, pots of cascading geraniums at the lock-keeper's gate, a blaze of wild roses against stone walls stained gray-green by the patina of ages, gypsy children playing by the water's edge…*

—My Journal, October 25, 1985

I sent postcards to all of my children against the backdrop of this slowly unfolding beauty.

*5 Rue Joseph Bara, Paris*

*I am now at my niece Roz's apartment bunking in the laundry room with a dyspeptic Scotch terrier called Bartholomew Cubbins. I like it better when I'm outside with my two great-nieces, eating at their favorite creperie, accompanying 7-year-old Marina onto crowded Rue Montparnasse in search of a Madonna poster but, most special of all, was the trip to Giverny to see my favorite artist's native setting.*

*With a minor in Art History from Barnard, I've had many chances over the years to see Monet on slides, in art books, and on museum walls, but nothing prepared me for the light at Giverny that day, misty and shimmering across the flowers and ponds. It was pure impressionism, distilled.*

With a case as serious as Cecily's, I never had illusions the path after McLean would be easy. Still, I wasn't prepared for a new unknown in her life.

In the summer of 1986, I saw a man heading upstairs to Cecily's apartment.

"I met him at Met State when I was visiting a friend," she told me. "He has nowhere to stay."

John Noble looked like his name: tall, dark, good looking. He was also taciturn, a school dropout, and a victim of an abusive father. It was hard for me to tell if he was naturally silent or clinically depressed.

When I asked Cecily, she brushed off the question with, "He's just very quiet, Mum."

"I'd like to meet him," I said.

"I don't think he'd like that."

She was in love with a stranger and planning to marry. I wasn't happy with her choice, but I was not ready for a battle I would surely lose. Charles felt the same way. "If we block the marriage, she'll just run off with him."

So we started premarital counseling with a rector at St. Anne's-in-the-Fields Church. Soon, Cecily was choosing bridesmaids for her wedding. Roz was maid of honor. John selected ushers from coworkers at the furniture moving company where he worked.

"No family? No friends? That's really weird," Chris remarked.

After the wedding at the church, we had a small reception on the wide lawn behind my condo. Cecily smiled with undiluted joy when Jay and Greg, her support team from McLean, arrived.

Later that year, Cecily gave birth to a seven-pound-one-ounce boy she named Sean. He captured my heart at first sight.

*Cecily holding Sean*

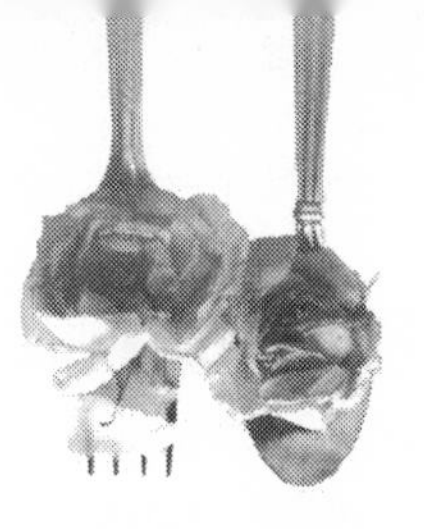

# chapter sixteen

In 1987, I met with other eating disorder professionals with a plan to link all the different eating disorder groups together as members of one new national organization. Across the country, eating disorder groups were proliferating, but each was operating in isolation. Services were getting duplicated and fundraising was difficult. We settled on a name for our new organization: National Eating Disorders Association.

I contacted my cousin, U.S. Congressman Hamilton Fish, who mailed out a "Dear Colleagues" letter to his peers telling them about our organization and the life-threatening eating disorder that afflicted so many. House Bill H.J.Res. 214 passed, and the week of October 23–29, 1989 became the first national step toward Eating Disorders Awareness and Prevention.

I met with Dr. Margo Maine in October 1998 when we both spoke at an eating-disorder panel in Columbus, Ohio. Her panel topic was fathers, a subject that was being seriously researched for the first time. Her book, *Father Hunger: Fathers, Daughters, and the Pursuit of Thinness*, was first published in 1991.[12]

Her hypothesis was that there was no cultural support for

active fathering before the seventies, that the cycle repeats when fathers are deprived of contact with their own fathers, so they are unable to nurture the next generation. These fathers stoically absorbed messages, such as "Don't cry," "Be tough," "Stand on your own two feet." Their emotional needs were not met, so they buy into the tragic patriarchal mythologies that separated them from their own emotional lives. They put emotional distance between themselves and their adolescent daughters. This emotionally distant father was not to blame. He was part of a cycle that kept him outside the emotional life of his family. He was a victim of the myths, family structures, and social patterns he couldn't fathom or control. I could have used the keen perspective of Dr. Maine during all those years of trying to understand my husband's withdrawal from our family.

My talk that day in Ohio was titled "Empowering the Mother," and I began with a sentence from Adrienne Rich's *Of Woman Born*: "The nurture of daughters in a patriarchal society calls for a strong sense of self-nurture in the mother." I spoke about myself and women I met through ABC. None of us asked or expected help from our husbands—and many, like me, feared confrontation. I spoke about the eating disordered daughter and the legacy she inherits: "Ignore your feelings and stay connected by doing for others." The sensitive daughter in such families can't see a route to self-worth, not in a society where girls feel it's unacceptable to show anger. Not in a society that lauds the emaciated body.

And not with the type of mother I was.

At the age of seventy-one, it was time for me to pass the reins of ABC to a younger leader. The board went into overdrive to fill my position.

That fall, I wrote my final newsletter to our membership:

*In May 1990, I told you about letting go and moving on; now it is October 1994, and I am still dealing with closure. It would seem I need a time management course, but first: a look back.*

*There have been many changes in the field of eating disorders since the founding of ABC in 1978. At that time, there were no resources in the area for family members, no support groups for the symptomatic, and only one pathway into an eating disorder. Today, these disorders are seen as complex and multi-determined, calling for an integrated treatment plan. Self-help or mutual empowerment groups, once looked on nervously by the professionals, are now generally viewed as an important adjunct to treatment. Theories, such as those on women's development, have opened up exciting avenues of research, but there is still much to be done, especially in the area of prevention and cure. Let's hold on to this dream, as we keep moving forward into the light.*

This final newsletter was difficult for me to write.

For years, my days and nights focused on trying to understand a disease that had turned my bright, sensitive, affectionate daughter to someone I barely recognized. One who became withdrawn, depressed, and irrationally obsessed with food, pushing herself to the edge of death. The more I discovered about the disease that consumed my daughter, the more I wanted to share my knowledge and feelings with other mothers and daughters facing a similar challenge. I never thought of myself as an "expert," just a mother with a sick child that society and the medical profession had yet to understand or remedy.

At the beginning, we were a small band of desperate

mothers and empathetic medical professionals who kept asking larger questions about complex family dynamics that pushed far beyond simple weight restoration programs. Along the way, our small group grew and grew, allowing new knowledge, understanding, and more humane treatments to reach vulnerable daughters and mothers who needed it the most. I never stopped learning or appreciating all the volunteers, doctors, therapists, mothers, and daughters who helped us contribute to a national network committed to successful eating disorder treatment.

On May 4, 1991, I was attending a conference at the Boston Park Plaza Hotel in honor of my work in the field of eating disorders. Dr. Alexandra Elliott, Anorexia Bulimia Care board member and chairperson for our conferences, gave her tribute:

"Growing up in the affluent but myopic, almost-schizoid world of New York City during the Great Depression, Patricia Warner was exposed to shifts in family circumstances. She was expected to sustain a façade of normalcy when the family's financial world was crumbling. The confusion and debility this caused was not unlike the confusion and unpredictability experienced by the eating disordered individual, or those struggling with other types of addiction. These were often burnt-out parents, who felt that, as Patricia had come to express in her own candid but non pejorative way, that the professionals who had assumed such huge roles in their lives had their own tunnel vision zeroed in on the anorexic mother."

Afterward, a group of us—volunteers, workshop members, the board—went to dinner at the Boston Park Plaza Hotel and toasted Anorexia Bulimia Care. The dinner put closure to an unforgettable period in my life. ABC has saved so many lives, including my daughter's, but it also saved me.

That night, I found a message on my pillow:

*I want you to know how proud I was of you today and how glad I will always be that you're my mother.*
*Forever with love,*
*Cecily*

A few months later, I received a letter from the White House. President George H. W. Bush was naming ABC one of his Thousand Points of Light, number 577:

"Since its founding in 1978 by two concerned parents, the ABC volunteers have helped thousands of eating disordered individuals through their wide range of outreach programs. Among them: Anorexia Bulimia Anonymous Groups, parents' workshops, monthly newsletters, and an informational hotline. The President salutes the volunteers of Anorexia Bulimia Care, Inc. for their community service efforts and for demonstrating his belief that, from now on in America, any definition of a successful life must include serving others."

This was the validation I never imagined I would hear. It finally gave me a new freedom to turn my attention to other members of the family and relish the time we had left together.

During this period, Charles was in his rented apartment in Cambridge, and my twin, Peter, was living with me in Lincoln. Peter knew almost all the walking trails edging our town. He loved to take coffee to the local police station and share stories about his maritime travels.

Peter was seventy-five years old when he died. We buried him next to our parents in the St. Philip's Church in the Highlands graveyard in Garrison, New York. The minister tapped down his urn with an umbrella as rain filled his open grave.

My brother would have enjoyed the northeast storm that day. I remember Charles taking him to Scollay Square and imitating his colorful sea speech, "Keep 'er between the buoys, Pat, or you'll go ashore at West Bank." Sadly, I did try to keep 'er between the buoys, Pete, but for too long lost my way.

On Charles's seventy-fifth birthday, Chris organized a Festschrift to honor the occasion. On the invitation, he wrote, *While my father is an enormously talented man, his greatest gift is the art of friendship.* Seventy-five letters from friends and family were included in the Festschrift; mine was the first:

> *I've been both center stage and in the wings of Charles's narrative, sometimes bemused by the defender of lost causes—the Restoration of the Monarchy and the 1974's Episcopal Prayer Book—other times fascinated by a man who can see the universe in the movements of mayflies on our sitting room screen door. So, happy birthday to my very best friend, and at times husband—with enduring love and all its mysteries, Pat.*

My nephew, Ricky, on the very last page of the Festschrift, had his own personal view of the honoree:

> *I've known my uncle 82% of my life. From the beginning, I was an instant partisan, mesmerized by his stories—of visiting the Hindenburg, pamphlets on beachheads, and Colonel Kavanaugh and the house on 62nd Street with its female dowagers—his mother and grandmother.*
>
> *An endearing, persistent characteristic of my uncle is his need to create and defend a civilized and ordered refuge within the many houses the Warner's have occupied. It has been a privilege to get his intellectual/historical perspective*

*while growing up in my branch of the family, where emotions often seem to drown out reason, and where history has to be tied to ancestors.*

By 1996, Charles had been living in Cambridge for almost fifteen years. His move away from our home might have singled a prelude to divorce, but it felt like a work-in-progress. He knew he had to get sober to live with me again.

At seventy-eight years of age, I didn't expect him to make a dramatic change, but I was aware of the changes in me and their effect on our marriage. I felt myself moving into a place of increasing self-awareness and authenticity. Even on days alone, I had reason to wake early to work on my manuscript, rather than fear being alone.

At the Harvard fiftieth reunion, sadness singed the festive atmosphere. Something was coming to an end. In Charles's apartment the night before, he showed me what he had submitted for the reunion's anniversary report. He wrote of the joy he got from shooting, fly fishing, and Iceland. He spoke of being happy with his family and circle of good friends, but the reunions always brought back memories of World War II and missing friends. Charles rarely spoke of the war, but I knew it had affected him deeply. In 1941, thirty-eight Harvard men died in battle, the highest mortality rate in any Harvard class since the Civil War.

The next morning, we went to a symposium to hear Dr. George Vaillant speak about his Grant Study, a decades-long study of the lives of sophomores from the Harvard classes of 1939–1944. Dr. Vaillant spoke about the undergraduates he interviewed from the class of 1941, the ways they matured, or didn't. Charles was restless when Dr. Vaillant discussed addictive behaviors. To age well physically, he said, "the single most important choice is to avoid heavy smoking and drinking before age 50, or to stop when young."

Charles reached for his pack of Salem's.

Two months later, Charles was rushed to Mt. Auburn Hospital with an angina attack. He recovered, but his doctors suggested he shouldn't live alone. Soon after, I received a phone call from my next-door neighbor. "Pat, this is Susan, your neighbor. Just thought I'd give you a heads-up if you know anyone who would like my condo."

The timing was perfect. Charles was finally coming home.

The day after he arrived, he noticed the books piled high on several dining room chairs. "Pat, do you still *only* read books on mental illness?"

"Well, I love mysteries. You know that."

"Then why not write a mystery?" he asked. Then, with the slightly crooked smile I always found endearing, he added, "Maybe a book on your OSS wartime experiences in Spain? Anyone will find *that* more interesting than eating disorders."

"Just accept me as I am."

Our acceptance of each other *had* changed over the years. Empathy and trust was now in place. I was no longer the *perfect* mother but a woman deeply affected by her own experiences—the fragility of a twin, the death of my first husband, and the disconnect between Charles and myself as we struggled with our daughter's illness.

By 1999, Cecily was very different from the patient doctors had given up on.

Her weight by then was about 115 pounds. Her bright smile

and honey-colored hair reflected the growth inside and outside of her.

That year, we visited McLean together to find a hospital that had changed, just as my own feelings toward it had softened. I started to forgive a hospital that has now eliminated many of the missteps that affected my daughter—the aversive practice of hydrotherapy, for example, which ended the year of Cecily's departure. And so, I slowly let go of the last remnants of my rage at McLean, believing doctors had done what they thought was right with what they knew at the time.

I wondered how St. Timothy's would handle a case like Cecily's today. So I wrote to the Director of Alumnae Development to ask her, and she sent me this:

*Dear Mrs. Warner,*

*You asked me to tell you how our school handles perceived eating disorders at the school. We are encouraged to watch for the warning signs of anorexia nervosa and bulimia. Some of the signs we look for are: students not eating at meals, pushing food around the plate, lethargic and/or secretive behavior, weight loss, meal time visits to the bathroom, over-exercising, and missing meals. Dormitory parents, faculty members, personal and class advisors, health center personnel and/or friends of the students may see signs.*

*Once we suspect that a student may be in trouble, an initial meeting is set up with the student and one or more of the following to express concern: her advisor, the Head of School, the Director of Counseling, a nurse or nurses from the school's Health Center. It depends on who has the closest rapport with the student. Contact is also made either by phone or in a meeting with the student's parents to express the same concern and to encourage them to seek medical help. Each case is treated on an individual basis—the school working intimately and confidentially with the family.*

*If the situation warrants, the school will, in consultation with the parents and medical personnel, make a decision based on the best interests of the child considering what health and personal services the school can and cannot supply.*

*Eating disorders are taken very seriously by the school.*

*You are to be commended for your years of work learning about and helping those with eating disorders. Health problems related to these disorders have disrupted and ruined far too many lives over too many years.*

*Very sincerely,*
*C. Y.*

On June 11, 2003, Cecily and I attended the opening of the Klarman Center at McLean. Dr. Steiner-Adair spoke about how patients can transition back to their communities and remain on a healthy regime of wellness.[13]

At the prededication lecture, Dr. Anne Becker, Director of Adult Eating and Weight Disorders from Massachusetts General Hospital, spoke about the arrival of television in the Fiji Islands and with it the appearance of eating disorder cases. Amazing that our toxic culture had been picked up and transported to such a remote area. In roughly three years of exposure to TV, two thousands years of cultural conditioning was erased, and the robust appetite of Fiji girls was no longer deemed acceptable.

I looked again at the mother-daughter connection and noted that clinicians today view mothers more kindly. "Certainly, they do not help," Dr. Janet Surrey wrote in 1984, "when they continue to blame the mothers for overinvolvement, enmeshment, and failure to tolerate separation."[14]

My world was brightening. I think of the Navajo proverb—*We are our ancestors*—and take heart. The generations that follow can learn from us, even from our poor choices and emotional blindness, but only if we speak in a clear and honest voice. Mothers of anorexics have a story to tell, but only if we reject our small roles in male-directed productions.

In early 2001, Charles was diagnosed with Alzheimer's, his short-term memory slowly unraveling. After a long goodbye of almost five years, Charles died on December 30, 2006 and was buried in the family graveyard in Garrison. I will always have the memories, wonderful memories.

"It's been a great ride, Old Wagon."

That was Charles's last complete sentence to me.

*Charles and I on vacation in Mexico*

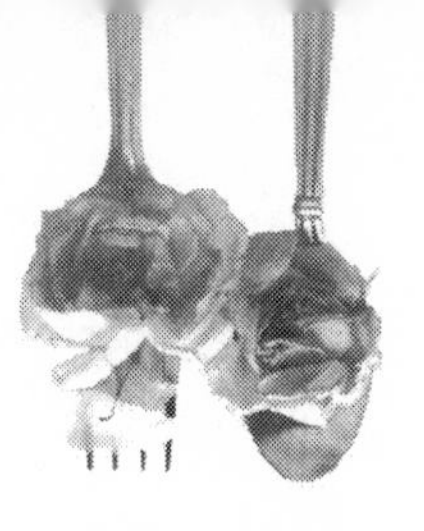

# chapter seventeen

Today, I look in the mirror and see a face worn and wrinkled and topped with a head of tousled white hair, like my mother's. It's then I hear Cecily's voice saying, *You're really real, Mum.* But am I strong enough for one more battle?

I stare at a framed photograph on my desk of a gray couple—Charles and I—sitting on the steps of a Mayan temple in the Yucatán. We look weathered and elemental, ravaged yet curiously softened by the passage of time. On the plane to Merida, I had said, "Wouldn't it be exciting to find a scaled antpitta? I can't picture a tailless bird."

Charles had replied, "I'm more interested in the violaceous trogon."

Looking at us with an objectivity I could have never managed three years ago, I think about our reasons for going on that trip. It allowed us to do the things we both love—ruins and bird life. But really it was to remove us geographically from the pain we felt over Cecily.

We did hear the Antpitta, a whistling series of cuckoos, and we did see the trogon, which is purplish. We came away with a tangible sense of life as a process, and the realization that there are many things that can never be fully understood. To know who were the builders of these lost cities and what the hieroglyphics on the stelae and stone lintels at Palenque say is surely as elusive an undertaking as charting the human condition. To accept that there is mystery brings its own kind of healing.

We took the long way home from Mexico to see two of our children, Rob and Nick, in Los Angeles. Rob was writing a movie about a female wrestler, and Nick had joined the blue-collar ranks as a journeyman machinist. It was wonderful to see both of them glowing with good health and established in their careers. Their main concern was for us and the toll that Cecily's disease was taking on us. "You're looking so tired, Mum," Nick had said.

Back home, I took out some old photo albums. Many of the photographs, bleached and grainy, were of people from ages long past—women in bathing dresses with long black stockings and men in boaters and blazers, grandparents, aunts, and uncles. I was looking for links and patterns, hoping to recapture the unique rhythms of an individual, a family, and the society that leaves a deep print on each human life.

I study a recent photograph of Rob—tall, dark, and fine-boned. He's concentrating on a spot along a California ridge. We had stopped on the drive to Santa Barbara for a picnic, and a breeze had come up as the smog hung high over the coastal hills. Rob was already older than his father was during our brief time together. It can be unsettling, this arithmetic of ages.

I turn the pages in my Moroccan leather album, flipping back to the beginning, to pages filled in by my mother, pictures of me smiling with my dog. Patterns: the people pleasers, the animal lovers—me and Cecily.

*Cecily sitting outside barn*

One particular lunch at home still lingers in my memory. When I finally sat down after cooking the meal, everyone had already cleaned their plates.

"Can I have another helping?" Charles asked.

Why didn't he see I hadn't eaten yet? Why didn't I say, "Wait until I've helped myself"?

Cecily quietly put what was left of the food onto my plate.

Through silences, both Cecily and I had become skilled in conflict avoidance. Like mother, like daughter—across generations.

The way feelings get handled all begins in one's family and spreads across generational boundaries. The way a great-grandfather does not talk about his dead wife, the way a grandmother waits to tell her children about her terminal cancer, the way a mother rarely speaks of the battle that killed her husband, the way a father avoids looking into the mystery of his own father. Grief, like anger and depression, gets buried.

Cecily, as a sensitive child growing up in such a home, might have gotten the message that this is the way to handle stress, that manipulating reality is the way to keep dark elements from overwhelming one's world.

With the best of intentions, parents can try to protect such a child from the hurt, not realizing that a display of honest emotions—outrage, grief, despair—can be the best learning experience. Sadly, cats do die. Life's traumas can't be orchestrated, nor can any child be strengthened by a predetermined plan. Chance and circumstance both play their parts, so the family legacy must be reexamined for each generation.

Until my daughter's anorexia showed me a different path, I was like most of the other mothers in my research study:

accommodating in the name of loyalty and peace, accepting unquestioningly the entire value system passed down across the generations.

I wish I had trusted my own instincts and considered the quality of her life. I now see long-term mental hospitalization as the worst option. Certainly, two years is a sufficiently lengthy trial period. Four years, God knows, is excessive.

I am still angry when I remember that no one on the staff at McLean ever thought to warn us about the dangers of institutionalization. No doctor ever hinted that it might be wise to leave the hospital early and risk the chance of death by suicide or medical complications than to stay on for years as a part of the woodwork.

I believe my daughter's path toward healing would have been shortened had I worked with Wellesley College's Stone Center group after her discharge from McLean. Relational-cultural theory, a core principle of the Stone Center Group, felt so right to me—that human beings grow through and toward connection, not separation.

Anorexia nervosa ravaged my daughter and tore relentlessly at the bonds that kept our family together. The hopelessness and despair I felt is familiar to the parents of anorexic children, yet each of our stories is unique.

According to Maureen Murdock, the memoirist, we lose our identity "in the silence of our mother's voice."[15] And yet, I recovered my voice, my true self, through the healing power of personal narrative. Cecily was my inspiration—all my children were allies—over the years.

I am so grateful to my daughter because she had the strength to overcome the disease and give *me* the strength to change.

Once she said, "Thanks, Mum, but I wish I didn't have to be so personally involved."

Looking back over the decades of disconnection, loss, and hope, I am sustained today by a sense of belonging and the knowledge that:

*The end of all our exploring*

*Will be to arrive where we started*

*And know the place for the first time.*

—T. S. Eliot, "Little Gidding"

*At home at Todd Pond*

## Acknowledgements

I want to thank, first and foremost, my beloved daughter, Cecily, who trusted her story with me. And to my son, Josh, who did so much to get the book published, and my son, Rob, who helped with the editing. A big thank-you also to my son, Chris, and granddaughter, Addie, who helped with the photos. Last but not least, I am very grateful to Laura Townsend Warner Wilson, my eldest grandchild, who transcribed my book and never complained about the countless revisions. The constant love and support of my entire family made this book possible. I thank each, and all, of you for your contributions and, most of all, love.

# Notes


1 Alistair Horne, *A Bundle from Britain* (London: Macmillan, 1993).
2 Beeson and McDermott, *Textbook of Medicine*, 11th ed. (Philadelphia: W. B. Saunders Co., 1963), 1716.
3 Currently used in Ireland, the United Kingdom, and other English-speaking countries, the acronym GP stands for "general practitioner," now known as a primary care physician in the US.
4 Hilde Bruch, MD, "Perils of Behavior Modification in Treatment of Anorexia Nervosa," *JAMA* 230, no. 2 (1974): 1419–1422.
5 Michele Siegel, PhD, Judith Brisman, PhD, Margot Weinshel, MSW, *Surviving an Eating Disorder: Strategies for Family and Friends* (New York: Harper & Row, 1988).
6 Robert Coles, MD, *The Mind's Fate* (Atlantic Monthly Press).
7 P. Garfinkel and D. Garner, *Anorexia Nervosa: A Multidimensional Perspective* (New York: Brunner/Mazel, 1982).
8 C. Park, *The Siege* (Atlantic Little Brown, 1967).
9 Simone de Beauvoir, *A Very Easy Death* (Putnam & Sons, 1966).
10 Alex Beam, *Gracefully Insane* (New York: Public Affairs, 2001).
11 Hilde Bruch, MD, *Eating Disorders, Anorexia Nervosa, and the Person Within* (New York: Basic Books, 1973).
12 Margo Maine, *Father Hunger: Fathers, Daughters, and the Pursuit of Thinness* (Carlsbad, CA: Gurze Books, 1991).
13 Catherine Steiner-Adair, "The Body Politic: Normal Female Adolescent Development and the Development of Eating Disorders" (EdD dissertation, Harvard Graduate School of Education, 1984).
14 Janet Surrey, PhD and Jean Baker Miller, *Stone Center: Work in Progress*, no. 9 (Training Institute at Wellesley College).
15 Maureen Murdock, *Unreliable Truth: On Memoir and Memory* (Seal Press, 2003).

## About the Author

Patricia Rosalind Warner has journeyed from New York City as a debutante in the late 1930s to spy and war widow in World War II to a mother of six children uprooted to college towns across the eastern and midwestern U.S. But her most challenging and transformative journey has been as the mother of an anorexic daughter. She cofounded of one of the first eating disorder groups in the U.S., the Anorexia Nervosa Aid Society. Her collection of writings and research on eating disorders is housed in a permanent collection at the Arthur and Elizabeth Schlesinger Library on the History of Women in America at Harvard University. She has eight grandchildren and lives in Massachusetts.

Made in the USA
Middletown, DE
29 May 2020